SQUADRONS!

No. 72

THE NEW ZEALAND DAY FIGHTER SQUADRONS IN EUROPE
- Nos 485 & 486 Squadrons -

PHIL H. LISTEMANN

ISBN: 978-2494471-28-3

Copyright

© 2025 Philedition - Phil Listemann

Colour profiles: Gaetan Marie/Bravo Bravo Aviation

GLOSSARY OF TERMS

PERSONEL :

(AUS)/RAF: Australian serving in the RAF
(BEL)/RAF: Belgian serving in the RAF
(CAN)/RAF: Canadian serving in the RAF
(CZ)/RAF: Czechoslovak serving in the RAF
(NFL)/RAF: Newfoundlander serving in the RAF
(NL)/RAF: Dutch serving in the RAF
(NZ)/RAF: New Zealander serving in the RAF
(POL)/RAF: Pole serving in the RAF
(RHO)/RAF: Rhodesian serving in the RAF
(SA)/RAF: South African serving in the RAF
(US)/RAF - RCAF : American serving in the RAF or RCAF

RANKS

G/C : Group Captain
W/C : Wing Commander
S/L : Squadron Leader
F/L : Flight Lieutenant
F/O : Flying Officer
P/O : Pilot Officer
W/O : Warrant Officer
F/Sgt : Flight Sergeant
Sgt : Sergeant
Cpl : Corporal
LAC : Leading Aircraftman

OTHER

ATA: Air Transport Auxiliary
CO : Commander
DFC : Distinguished Flying Cross
DFM : Distinguished Flying Medal
DSO : Distinguished Service Order
Eva. : Evaded
ORB : Operational Record Book
OTU : Operational Training Unit
PoW : Prisoner of War
PAF: Polish Air Force
RAF : Royal Air Force
RAAF : Royal Australian Air Force
RCAF : Royal Canadian Air Force
RNZAF : Royal New Zealand Air Force
SAAF : South African Air Force
s/d: Shot down
Sqn : Squadron
† : Killed

CODE-NAMES - OFFENSIVE OPERATIONS - FIGHTER COMMAND

CIRCUS:

Bombers heavily escorted by fighters, the purpose being to bring enemy fighters into combat.

RAMROD:

Bombers escorted by fighters, the primary aim being to destroy a target.

RANGER:

Large formation freelance intrusion over enemy territory with aim of wearing down enemy fighters.

RHUBARB:

Freelance fighter sortie against targets of opportunity.

ROADSTEAD:

Dive bombing and low level attacks on enemy ships at sea or in harbour

RODEO:

A fighter sweep without bombers.

SWEEP:

An offensive flight by fighters designed to draw up and clear the enemy from the sky.

THE NEW ZEALAND DAY FIGHTER SQUADRONS IN EUROPE

Shortly after Britain's declaration of war, supported on the same date by Australia and New Zealand, and Canada a week later, the British Government asked Commonwealth countries to supply partially trained aircrew for the expansion of the RAF. In those years prior to the war an allocation of men from the Dominions had been offered Short Service, or Permanent, Commission in the RAF, but the speed with which the Nazis had overrun Poland, made it clear that large numbers of airmen would be needed urgently. In November 1939, the Ottawa (Canada) Conference formulated the setting-up of the Empire Air Training Scheme (EATS) to train aircrew to a uniform standard in each of the Dominions previously mentioned, and subsequently South Africa, which was already operating a scheme, and Rhodesia.

Desirous of exercising some control over its own nationals, which was not the case for those who had joined up prior to the war, Canada obtained, via Article XV, an agreement that their aircrew would be gathered together in national squadrons, to serve alongside the permanent units of the RAF. For operational and administrative reasons Australia and New Zealand were reluctant to establish and maintain RAAF or RNZAF squadrons in Britain so eventually it was decided that units formed in the RAF would be identified with them.

In order to distinguish those units created under Article XV the RAF reserved a block of numbers commencing with 400 which was allocated to them. The RCAF squadrons were to start with 400, the RAAF, 450 and the RNZAF, 485. From the start aircrew were paid at the rates of pay in force in their respective countries, and depended on the RAF for aircraft and logistical support. The operational deployment was to be determined by the RAF, even though respective Governments of each of the Dominions retained an overview on their airmen. Some existing squadrons were re-numbered in the new series to avoid confusion with established RAF units. As an example, No. 1 Squadron RCAF, which was sent to support Great Britain in 1940, was subsequently re-numbered No. 401 (RCAF) Squadron. The policy behind Article XV Squadrons provided a greater national identity to those countries who were able to identify themselves in their title e.g. No. 485 (NZ) Squadron. Initially the RAF supplied the vast majority of the ground personnel for most of the Commonwealth squadrons. The aircrew posted to these squadrons represented only some, and not all, of that particular country's nationals. Indeed, almost every squadron in the RAF at some time or another had members amongst their ranks from all of the Dominions - aircrew were sent where there was the greatest need for them.

In the beginning the authorities attempted to relocate serving RAF officers to those newly formed squadrons from their Dominions. However, this was not always possible or practical, especially where senior positions needed to be filled. As a result, British or other nationals frequently filled the vacancies in these squadrons. Regrettably friction between nationalities sometimes occurred, although this was not a major problem. The posting or replacement of certain personnel would generally defuse such situations.

By the end of the war Article XV Squadrons had proved that they were equal to the best that the RAF had produced and had no need to be envious of their British counterparts. Not only had they achieved impressive operational records but they gave the Dominions a renewed confidence and pride in their military ability. As far as the New Zealanders were concerned, two day fighter squadrons were formed in UK, Nos 485 and 486, the latter being, however, initially formed for the night-fighting role. The New Zealanders would have a third day fighter squadron, No. 488, which was formed at Singapore in 1941 (*see SQUADRONS! 33*) but it didn't survive the military disaster that follow the Japanese invasion of December 1941, and would be re-formed in UK in 1942 as a night fighter squadron. When war broke out, many New Zealanders were already serving with the RAF, and some of them became highly respected wing leaders even before the formation of Nos 485 and 486 Squadrons took place, like MV Blake, AC Deere, PG Jameson or later on, CF Gray or ED Mackie.

The third and last New Zealander day fighter squadron formed under Article XV was No. 488 which briefly saw action in the Far East flying Brewster Buffaloes and Hawker Hurricanes. Within a couple of weeks it was totally wiped out and eventually re-formed in the UK as a night fighter squadron in June 1942.

'Jamie' Jameson left New Zealand in January 1936 his intention being to secure a Short Service Commission with the RAF. In December, having completed his training, he joined No. 46 Squadron initially flying Gauntlets, and then Hurricanes, and early in 1939 had become a flight commander. During May 1940 the squadron was deployed to Norway where, on 28 May, Jameson shared in the destruction of two Do26s, secured in a fjord, and the next day he shot down a Ju88. On the 7 June, following the order to evacuate Norway, the squadron's Hurricanes were flown aboard the carrier HMS *Glorious*. The following day, the carrier was sunk by the German battle-cruisers *Scharnhorst* and *Gneisenau*. Jameson was rescued, after 3 days on a Carley float, and returned to the UK where he recovered. Awarded the DFC in July 1940, he was given command of No. 266 Squadron in mid- September 1940. Although fully operational it wasn't until April 1941 that he began scoring again, claiming three confirmed victories in three months, two of which were night interceptions. He was promoted and in June was appointed Wing Commander Flying of the Wittering Wing, with which he made a further three claims. He was awarded a Bar to his DFC in October 1941 and from that date became Wing Leader of the West Malling Wing at the head of which on 19 August 1942 over Dieppe, he shot down a Fw190. In December 1942 he became Wing Leader of the North Weald Wing, making four more claims. These elevated his score to eight aircraft destroyed, two probably destroyed, one of which was shared, and three damaged, plus the share in the two flying boats. He was awarded the DSO during March and in May joined HQ, No.11 Fighter Group. In July 1944 Jameson, a group Captain, took command of No. 122 Wing, 2TAF, holding this position until it was disbanded in September 1945. He continued serving in the RAF until August 1960 when he retired as an Air Commodore.

Supermarine Spitfire Mk II P7315
No. 266 Squadron
Squadron Leader PG Jameson
Wittering (UK), September 1940

Minden Vaughan BLAKE
RAF No. 36095

Minden Blake, a New Zealander from Newman, sailed for the UK in November 1936 to enlist in the RAF. He started his training the following month, and was granted a Permanent Commission in March 1937. By the outbreak of war he was already a Flight Commander serving with No. 17 Squadron on Hurricanes. In April 1940 he was sent to Ternhill as a flying instructor but in August, when the need for fighter pilots became vital, he was posted to No. 238 Squadron. The squadron was minus a CO and he took over, in an acting capacity, although still a Flight Lieutenant. He opened his score on 21 August by destroying a Ju88 and added three more bombers, two of which were shared with fellow pilots, within a month. He had been with the squadron about five weeks, when he was given command of No. 234 Squadron. His score continued to increase and in December he was awarded the DFC. During 1941 he scored five more kills, but was himself shot down on 10 July, and had to ditch into the Channel. He managed to paddle clear of the French Coast and, after approximately 10 hours, was rescued not far from the English coastline. He returned briefly to 234 Squadron but, at the end of July, took charge as Wing Leader of No. 2 (Polish) Wing at Exeter. Two months later he became Wing Leader of the Portreath Wing, and received a DSO in August 1942. On 19 August, while leading the Wing over Dieppe, he made his last claim, a Fw190 destroyed, before being shot down himself and parachuting into the sea, with eye injuries. This time he was picked up by a German patrol boat and taken back to France. While on route to prison camp he jumped from a moving train and was badly injured. He was recaptured, finishing the war as a PoW. Released in May 1945, he remained with the RAF until retirement in January 1958. His score is made up of thirteen confirmed victories, five being shared, and one damaged.

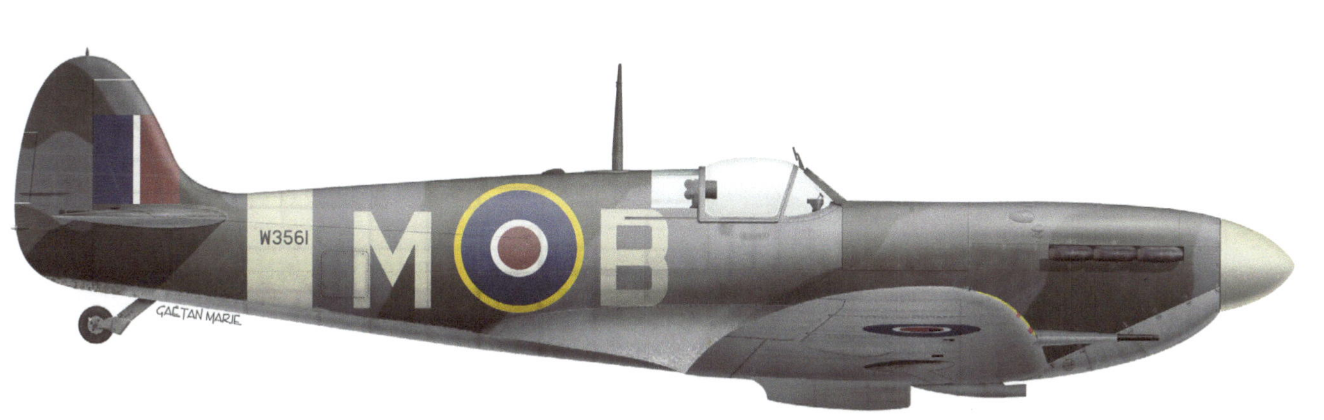

Supermarine Spitfire Mk VB W3561
Portreath Wing
Wing Commander MV Blake
Redhill (UK), spring 1942

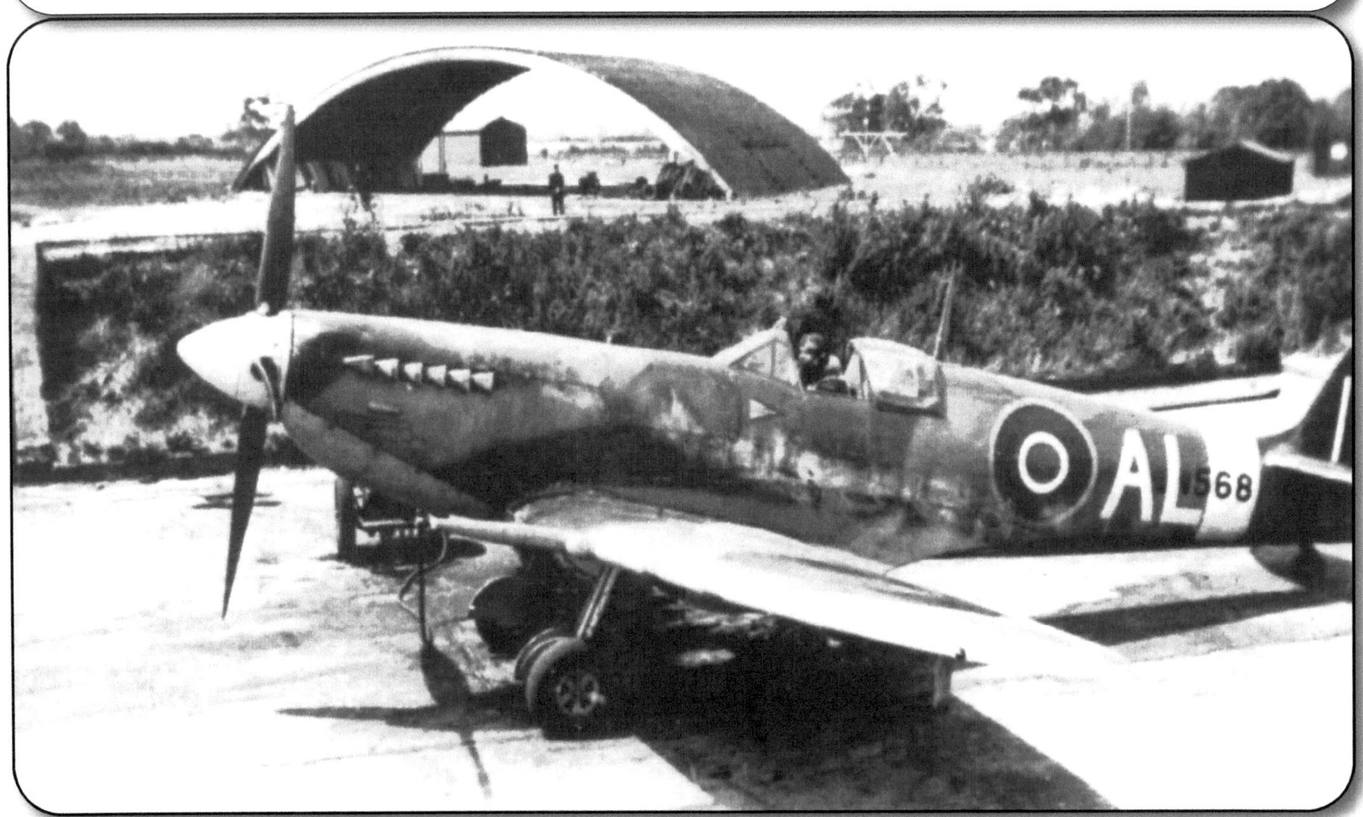

During the summer of 1942, Blake flew Spitfire V W3561baring his initials 'M-B'. He was piloting this plane when he was shot down on 19 August 1942. *(Andrew Thomas)*

Wing Commander Al Deere's Spitfire Mk IX, EN568/AL in the spring of 1943. *(Andrew Thomas)*

Alan Christopher Deere

RAF No. 40370

'Al' Deere travelled to England in September 1937 to join the RAF on a short service commission. On completion of his training, he was posted to No. 54 Squadron in August 1938, flying Gladiators. When war broke, he was still with the unit which was now flying Spitfires. It was during May 1940 over the French coast, that Deere opened his score claiming two Bf109s on 23 May. By the end of the month, he had already reached ace status and had become a flight commander. He had also been shot down himself. He was awarded the DFC in June, scoring at a good clip during the Battle of Britain, and by the end of August, his total of confirmed kills had risen to 15, including three which were shared with other pilots. During this period, he was shot down twice more, once by a Spitfire, and crashed twice, once after colliding with a Me109, and once after being caught by bombers while taking off. The squadron was withdrawn for rest early in September, and he received a Bar to his DFC that same month. His tour ended in January 1941, and he was off operations until May when he was posted to No. 602 (City of Glasgow) Squadron as a flight commander, taking command of the Squadron in August. He led the unit until January 1942, and was again rested. In May 1942 he took command of No. 403 (RCAF) Squadron leading it until August, when he was spelled. He returned to operations in February 1943, securing a brief attachment to No. 611 (West Lancashire) Squadron, before becoming Wing Leader of Biggin Hill Wing in March, a position he was to hold until September. His final claim was on 14 July, which brought his total victories to eighteen confirmed (three being shared), seven unconfirmed or probable (one being shared) and six damaged. He had awarded the DSO during June 1943 and in May 1944, assumed command of No. 145 Wing, before joining staff at 84 Group. Post-war Deere was granted a Permanent Commission with the RAF, retiring in 1967 as an Air Commodore.

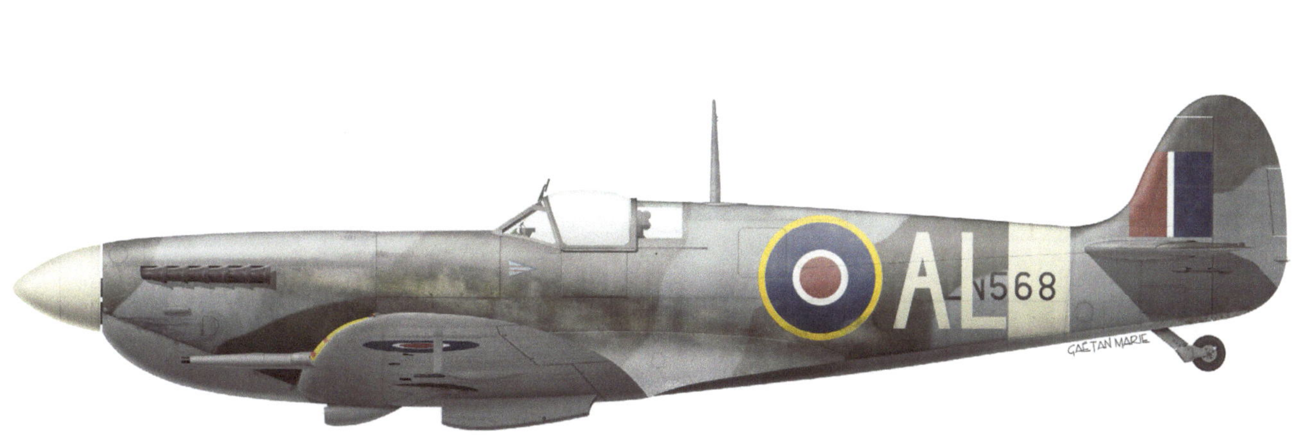

Supermarine Spitfire Mk IXB EN568
Biggin Hill Wing
Wing Commander AC Deere
Biggin Hill (UK), spring 1943

Colin Falkland GRAY
RAF No. 41844

Colin Gray tried twice to enlist in the RAF before being accepted on a third attempt in September 1938. During December he set sail for the UK to commence training, upon the completion of which he joined No. 54 Squadron, on Spitfires, in November 1939. He opened his score on 24 May 1940 when he claimed a Bf109 as probable near Calais. Further successes followed, during the summer of 1940, leading to the award of a DFC in August. When the squadron was withdrawn for rest, early in September, he was among the most successful RAF fighter pilots at that time with 17 confirmed victories, one being shared. In December 1940 he was posted to No. 43 Squadron, as a flight commander, but a month later transferred back to 54 Squadron in the same capacity. In June 1941 he took charge of a flight in No. 1 Hurricane Squadron, participating in both day and night operations. He received a Bar to his DFC in September 1941, shortly before being ordered to take charge of No. 403 (RCAF) Squadron. At short notice this was changed to No. 616 (South Yorkshire) Squadron, which he led until February 1942, when he was rested.

Returning to operations in September he was briefly attached to No. 485 (NZ) Squadron before transferring to No. 64 Squadron, where he flew the first Spitfire Mk.IXs. He took over the squadron at the beginning of November but towards the end of December was sent to North Africa, and in January 1943 took command of No. 81 Squadron. He distinguished himself over Tunisia, while flying Spitfire IXs, making nine claims of the various categories, at the head of his squadron. In May he was awarded the DSO and later promoted Wing Leader of No. 322 Wing, which moved to Malta for the Invasion of Sicily. His final claim, two Ju52s on the 25 July, brought his total to 29 confirmed victories, two being shared, 10 probables, four being shared, and 12 damaged. Therefore he became the top scoring New Zealand fighter pilot of WW2. His second tour ended during September 1943 and soon after he returned to the UK, where he received a second Bar to his DFC. He recommenced operations in July 1944 as WingCo Flying of the Detling Wing, and a month later of the Lympne Wing, where he flew anti-V1 missions. He held this position until January 1945 and continued to serve with the RAF post-war, retiring in April 1961.

Supermarine Spitfire Mk XIV RM787
Lympne Wing
Wing Commander CF Gray
Lympne (UK), October 1944

Above, Wing Commander Gray's Spitfire XIV, RM787 at Lympne in October 1944.
(Andrew Thomas)

When Mackie became the Wing Commander of 122 Wing, he acquired a new Tempest, SN228 which was coded 'EDM' and his scoreboard made at the time of 24 swatiskas and a single Italian marking. At some time in the summer of 1945, a 122 Wing badge was added to the fin of SN228, bearing the original title of the unit '122 Airfield Headquarters'. The spinner was repainted, most probably in yellow.
(CT Collection)

'Rosie' Mackie joined the RNZAF in January 1941 and, upon completion of his training, arrived in the UK during the summer of 1941. Following OTU, he was posted to 485 (NZ) Squadron in August 1941. He made his first claim on 26 March 1942, sharing a Bf109 destroyed. He volunteered to serve in North Africa and, in January 1943, joined 243 Squadron in March, becoming a flight commander in April. The Tunisian campaign was raging at the time and, after a promising debut in UK, Mackie's score exploded during the spring of 1943. In May, he was awarded the DFC and in June he was promoted to command the squadron. More successes followed over Sicily and Italy and he added a Bar to his DFC in September. In November, he was posted out to command 92 Squadron until the end of February 1944 when he left Italy to return to the UK for a rest.

He returned to operations in December 1944, joining 274 Squadron as supernumerary squadron leader, flying Tempests. In January, he left 274 to command 80 Squadron, leading the unit until April when he was promoted to wing leader of 122 Wing, the only 2TAF wing formed with Tempest-equipped squadrons, where he would make his final claims, the very last in the air on 15 April. He continued to lead the wing until September by which time he had been made a Companion of the DSO (in May). His final score was 23 confirmed victories (three shared), two probables and eleven damaged.

Hawker Tempest Mk V SN228
No. 122 Wing
Wing Commander ED Mackie
B.152/Fassberg (Germany), April-May 1945

Hawker Tempest Mk V SN228
No. 122 Wing
Wing Commander ED Mackie
B.152/Fassberg (Germany), summer 1945

Victories - confirmed or probable claims: 95.0

Number of sorties: *ca.* 10,000

First operational sortie:
12.04.41

Last operational sortie:
07.05.45

Total aircraft written-off: 84

Aircraft lost on operations: 73
Aircraft lost in accidents: 11

Squadron code letters:

OU

COMMANDING OFFICERS

S/L Marcus W.B. KNIGHT	RAF No. 37408	(NZ)/RAF	...	23.11.41
S/L Edward P. WELLS	NZ39950	RNZAF	23.11.41	05.05.42
S/L Reginald J.C. GRANT	NZ391352	RNZAF	05.05.42	20.03.43
S/L Reginald W. BAKER	NZ401748	RNZAF	20.03.43	01.07.43
S/L John M. CHECKETTS (*s/d, Eva.*)	NZ403602	RNZAF	01.07.43	06.09.43
S/L Martin R.D. HUME	NZ405335	RNZAF	06.09.43	21.02.44
S/L John B. NIVEN	RAF No. 109061	RAF	21.02.44	15.09.44
S/L John G. PATTISON	NZ39931	RNZAF	15.09.44	21.02.45
S/L Keith J. MACDONALD	NZ40981	RNZAF	21.02.45	16.07.45
S/L Stanley F. BROWNE	NZ411853	RNZAF	16.07.45	26.08.45

SQUADRON USAGE

New Zealand, via the Empire Air Training Scheme, raised its first squadron, 485, on 1 March 1941 at Driffield in Yorkshire. Chosen to lead the squadron was S/L M.C.B. Knight, a New Zealander serving in the RAF since 1935. The two flight commanders were also Kiwis enlisted in the RAF: Flight Lieutenants F.N. Brinsden and J.C. Martin. All were Battle of Britain veterans. The squadron worked up on Spitfire Mk.Is and was declared operational by mid-April. On 12 April, a series of convoy patrols and scrambles were undertaken but all were uneventful. The old Spitfires were progressively replaced by Mk.IIs in early June 1941, the last of the 285 sorties recorded by the Mk I being flown on 22 June. All left soon after but two which was wrecked during a training flight on 5 May, followed by another one four days later during a convoy patrol. Sergeant J.K. Porteous saw the engine of his Spitfire to catch fire in flight; he left the convoy and made for land and managed to make a wheels-up landing at Buckton. As there was no real difference between the marks, the pilots easily converted within a day and continued operational duties with barely an interruption. The first fifteen had arrived by 15 June. On 2 June, 485 carried out eighteen sorties across several convoy patrols. The change of mount brought luck for the Kiwis. Flight Lieutenant Brinsden and P/O R. Barrett were ordered to protect a convoy of thirty ships 12-15 miles off Hornsea late in the afternoon. After an hour, when flying below cloud, the section sighted an enemy aircraft (later identified as a Ju88) emerge from cloud and about 400 feet above. The Junkers probably saw the two New Zealanders as it immediately dropped its bombs some distance from the nearest ship and took violent evasive action, turning and climbing into cloud cover. Brinsden attacked and fired a burst, with full deflection, from about 250 yards, and followed it up with another short, but ineffective, burst from astern. Return fire from the Junkers was experienced and Brinsden received two bullets in the glycol header tank and oil cooler. Pilot Officer Barrett followed his leader in the attack and fired two short bursts. While he also experienced return fire, he was not hit, but could not claim to have damaged the German bomber. The Ju88 managed to disappear into cloud and contact was lost. The pair was replaced by F/L Martin and Sgt W.H. Russell who also encountered a Ju88, but the situation was less favourable and only Martin managed to fire two ineffective bursts. Another pair, Pilot Officers G.H. Francis and H.H. Thomas, arrived to continue to cover the convoy. They were patrolling at 1500 feet when they saw a Ju88 emerge from cloud about 500 feet above and on their left. The German crew saw the Spitfires as well and immediately turned to the left and climbed for cloud. It was followed by Francis who fired a short burst from 300 yards before closing in with a two second burst. Sergeant Thomas

485 Squadron founding members, Driffield, Spring 1941.
Rear, left to right: Corporal French (ground-crew), Sgt D.S. McGregor (†09.05.44 - 598 Sqn), P/O R. Barrett (†07.05.44 - 65 Sqn), P/O W.A. Middleton (†27.08.41), P/O G.H. Francis, P/O A.G. Shaw (a New Zealander in the RAF), F/L J.C. Martin (†27.08.41 - 222 Sqn, New Zealander in the RAF), S/L M.W.B. Knight, F/L F.N. Brinsden, P/O P.S. McBride, P/O A.G. McIntyre, Corporal T.G. Smith (ground-crew), LAC Bongard (groundcrew), LAC Erridge (groundcrew), Corporal Murray (ground-crew), LAC MacGibbon (groundcrew).
Front, left to right: Sgt George (ground-crew), LAC Neville (ground-crew), LAC Martin (ground-crew), Sgt H.L. Thomas, Sgt R.J. Bullen (†23.06.41), Sgt W.V. Crawford-Compton, Sgt J. Maney (†24.07.41), Sgt J.K. Porteous, Sgt A.B. Smith, Sgt H.N. Sweetman, Sgt K.D. Cox (†18.06.41).
(Paul Sortehaug)

followed, firing a long burst, and strikes were seen along the fuselage. Some of his bullets struck aft the cockpit and pieces were seen flying off. That was all they could do as the Ju88 found safety in the cloud and contact was lost. It was claimed as damaged, however, to open 485's score. Later, the final pair, the CO and P/O A.G. McIntyre, the latter being a New Zealander serving in the RAF began their patrol. At about 22.25, as darkness set in, a Ju88 was sighted below cloud about one mile to the right. Squadron Leader Knight immediately attacked and observed strikes along the left side of the fuselage as well as the wing roots and engine. Return fire was experienced, but was silenced at once. The Junkers entered cloud with its left engine on fire and smoke issuing from the right engine. Nothing else could be done, but later on the naval escort reported a Ju88 had crashed into the sea. It was the squadron's first confirmed kill of the war. Operational activity continued during the month, but no further encounters occurred. However, 485 lost two pilots in June. Sergeant K.D. Cox was killed doing aerobatics on the 18th. His Spitfire was seen to crash from 800 feet as he was performing a slow roll. The second loss occurred a few days later on the 23rd when Sgt R.J. Bullen was posted missing. That day 485 carried its first Wing patrol over the French coast. Bullen became separated from the other three in his section and reported he was continuing the patrol alone. While returning from the French coast at 7000 feet, he was found being attacked by Bf109s from astern. Hit, the Spitfire ended up on its back as it spun towards the sea with clouds of white and black smoke coming from the engine. During the final week of June, the nature of the operational activity turned to the offensive and no less than four more Wing sweeps were flown, but all were uneventful. By the end of the month, the Spitfire Mk.IIs in service with the squadron were P7438/Q, P7566/Z, P7605/N, P7621/Y, P7697/B, P7758/F, P7773/D, P7785, P7788/E, P7821, P7822/A, P7916, P7964, P7974/L, P7908, P7961, P7975/R, P7977/U, P7986/G and P8025/P.

After completing just over 200 sorties in June, July would see close to 450 more flown during the month. This increase in activity was the consequence of the move from Leconsfield to Redhill at the beginning of the month. The move was also accompanied with a change of leadership as P/O E.P. Wells had succeeded F/L Martin as A Flight Leader a couple of days before. On 3 July 485 carried out two operations, one in the morning and one in the afternoon, but both proved uneventful. Another was flown the next day, along with some convoy patrols, but the enemy was not engaged. An engagement finally took place on the 5th during an escort for three Stirlings to Lille. The squadron took off shortly after midday and, while over Lille about one hour later, now F/L Wells saw a Bf109 make a very faint-hearted pass at the bombers and continue its dive at high speed, passing near Wells and his wingman, P/O R.H. Strang. Wells immediately moved into a good position and, allowing for full deflection, fired a quick burst before following the flee-

The squadron's presentation Spitfires, paid for by funds raised in New Zealand, lined-up in early September 1941. The new camouflage scheme had been just introduced in Fighter Command. In the forefront, AB918/OU-Y 'Wellington I'. *(via P. Sortehaug)*

ing aircraft down. Wells fired one more short burst and then broke away out of the vertical dive. The German pilot was seen to bale out soon after. Proceeding home, and trying to catch up with the rest of the squadron in the distance, Wells noticed several Bf109s flying towards them immediately above. He called out a warning and at the same time turned slightly and saw two more Bf109s flying a bit below in wide abreast formation. He decided to close in on the nearest one and did so without much difficulty. Apparently unobserved, Wells was able to fire a two second burst from 250 yards and slightly to one side. The Bf109 started a climbing turn, which Wells was able to follow easily, before another two second burst blew off the hood and black smoke began pouring out. As the Bf109 was pulling up higher, Wells delivered a third two second burst from very close range. The German pulled up even steeper, stalled and started to spin. As he flicked over, Wells saw flames coming from the sides of the fuselage which was probably burning petrol pouring out of the stricken airframe. Wells was attacked at that moment so had to evade violently, but he eventually returned home to make a double claim. The New Zealanders sustained no loss. The 6th and 7th were also busy with escorts and patrols, as were the 8th and 9th, but during the Circus on the 8th Sgt W.H. Hendry was posted missing. He was last seen off Gravelines. That same afternoon, P/O C. Stewart, a New Zealander serving in the RAF redressed the balance when he sent a Bf109 into the Channel off Calais during a coastal cover patrol led by W/C J.R.A. Peel. Sadly, Stewart did not have the opportunity to score again as he was posted missing three days later after a fighter sweep in almost the same area. The squadron was attacked by six enemy fighters at 23,000 feet. Stewart was last seen over the Straits of Dover. The pressure was maintained with close to 200 sorties carried out between the 12th and the 23rd, but 485 would have to wait until the 24th to report success. That day, while escorting bombers to Cherbourg, F/L E.P. Wells destroyed a Bf109 near the town, his fifth confirmed victory (he had achieved his first two with 41 Squadron), but this was balanced by the loss of Sgt J. Maney. He was seen being shot down and descending safely under his parachute about 15 miles north of Cherbourg. Despite this, he and his aircraft were lost without trace. The last week of July was less intense and 485 only performed patrols during which nothing of importance happened. A new B Flight leader, F/L S.C. Norris, assumed his role from the 22nd. This low rate of operations continued during early August with just some Rhubarbs flown. It was not until the 5th that the squadron returned over the continent on a Circus that could not be completed because of bad weather. The next day, 485 performed a cover patrol off Dungeness without incident. On the 7th, 485 participated in *Circus* 67 during which Sgt C.S.V. Goodwin failed to return. He was later reported as a PoW. That day, the Wing was engaged over Saint-Omer and Goodwin was shot down by Fw190s, baling out of his flaming Spitfire. He was captured with burns to his wrists and face, very common injuries as these areas were often the pilot's only exposed skin, and spent some time in hospital before being transferred to a PoW camp. The squadron seemed to be running out of luck. While the two following fighter sweeps over the continent were eventful, the Circus that followed on the 12th saw two more pilots lost. Sergeant G.M. Porter, a New Zealander serving in the RAF was killed and Sgt W.H. Russell joined Goodwin at the hospital in Saint-Omer. He was so severely injured he had to have an arm amputated and was eventually repatriated in 1943. Two days later, the squadron began to re-equip with Spitfire Mk.Vs, but would continue to fly the Mk.II for a little while longer. On 16 August a mixed force, led by S/L Knight, flew an offensive sweep first thing in the morning and, around midday, acted as support cover to *Circus* 74. In the course of this operation various engagements developed and Sgt

L.J. Frecklington, flying a Mk.II, claimed a Bf109 probably destroyed near Cap Gris-Nez while Sgt L.P. Griffiths, who was also flying a Mk.II, claimed another as damaged. A third claim was made by F/L Wells, but he was flying a Mk.V. The re-equipment continued rapidly over the next few days and the last Spitfire II sorties were carried out on the morning of the 19th during *Circus* 82. An engagement took place on the return journey before the squadron reached the French coast. Sergeant J.D. Rae saw a 485 Spitfire (Sgt K.C.M. Miller) being attacked and mortally hit. It was last seen diving with glycol streaming behind. He then saw the Bf109 begin to manoeuvre to repeat his attack on Rae. A violent dogfight ensued at the end of which Rae was able to fire a two second burst. The Bf109 spun into the ground out of control. This was revenge for Miller who was reported as killed in action. An evening Lysander escort was performed entirely with Spitfire Mk.Vs, so Rae's victory proved a fitting end for the squadron's time with the Mk.II. In all, 485 flew about 800 sorties on their old mounts.

Regarding the Spitfire Mk V, the New Zealanders took charge of aircraft funded by various subscriptions in New Zealand. Indeed, there had been a certain public fascination for the Spitfire, resulting from the Battle of Britain, and this was something the authorities seized upon. A fund was set up, to which New Zealand and its Pacific Island protectorates could subscribe, to purchase Presentation aircraft for a nationally identifiable squadron. The amount raised, £126,000 Sterling, funded more than twenty Spitfires, mainly named after the country's provinces, and these were allocated to 485 Squadron. By mid-August, 485 had the following Spitfires on charge: P8786, W3406/H, W3454, W3500, W3527/M, W3577/P, W3578, W3579/Q, W3643/C, W3652/V, AB784/N, AB788/T, AB806, AB853, AB860/U, AB870/Z and AB918/Y.

The squadron carried out its first operation with the new mark, escorting medium bombers to Boulogne Harbour, on 14 August. However, this op was achieved with a mixed force of Spitfire IIs and Vs. In the meantime, during an offensive sweep early on the morning of the 16th, F/L E.P. Wells and Sgt L.P. Griffith each claimed a Bf109 damaged east of Dunkirk and, after lunch, Sgt L.J. Frecklington sent a lone Bf109 spinning down, shedding debris, in the vicinity of Saint-Omer. However, as only Wells was flying a Spitfire V, he therefore made the squadron's first claim on the new aircraft. He distinguished himself three days later on the 19th by claiming two more Messerschmitts, one destroyed and another damaged, near Marquise and remained the unit's only pilot to score with the Mk.V as all the other claims that day were made by pilots flying Mk.IIs. The first loss was recorded on the 27th when P/O W.A. Middleton fell to a pair of Bf109s in the vicinity of Saint-Omer during an escort sortie. A further two successes were claimed on the 29th for the loss of a Spitfire. The New Zealanders were severely engaged while escorting bombers to Hazebrouck, but they got the advantage over the Bf109s with one aircraft destroyed each to F/L Stan Norris, the English Battle of Britain veteran, and Sgt H.N. Sweetman. On the debit side, Sgt Griffith's aircraft was hit by flak, but he was fortunate as he was swiftly rescued after having to jump out over the Channel during the return flight. August ended with an uneventful sweep over Saint-Omer. During the month 485 had logged 320 sorties (half were flown on Spitfire Vs). In September, activity was cut by half, with about 150 sorties carried out, most being escorts. That was the case on the 2nd, acting as cover for bombers attacking a convoy off Ostend, followed

A line-up of several New Zealand presentation Spitfire Vs, with W3528/OU-C in the foreground, at Redhill in September 1941. Ahead of the cockpit, the inscription 'WDFUNZ/Levin' stood for 'Women's Division of the Farmer's Union of NZ'. Behind, the CO's Spitfire, AB870/Z, was named 'Hawkes Bay I/Dannevirke'. Far behind, the Spitfire coded OU-H was W3406 and named 'Auckland III'. *(via P. Sortehaug)*

An informal photo of a group of pilots at Redhill in 1941. On the aircraft: F/L R.H. Strang, a New Zealander serving in the RAF (†25.01.42), Sgt I.J. McNeil, Sgt L.J. Frecklington, P/O G.H. Francis, and Sgt W.M. Krebs (†26.03.42). Standing: P/O H.W. McLeod, a Canadian and future RCAF ace (†27.09.44 as OC 443 Sqn), Sgt E.A. Cochrane (†02.03.43 with 146 Sqn in Burma), Sgt L.P. Griffith, P/O W.V. Crawford-Compton, a New Zealander serving in the RAF, S/L M.W. Knight (OC), Sgt A.S. Kronfeld, a Samoan, and P/O D.T. Clouston. Sitting: Sgt J.D. Rae (PoW 22.08.43), P/O R. Barrett (†17.05.44 with 65 Sqn) and Sgt H.N. Sweetman.

by another to Bethune two days later and then ten days of inactivity. After an ineffective fighter sweep on the 16th, 485 returned to escort duties twice on the 17th. While the first Circus of the morning was achieved without incident, during the afternoon's escort F/L Wells claimed a Bf109 probably destroyed, and the following afternoon four more claims against Bf109s were made for the loss of a pilot while escorting Blenheims to Rouen (*Circus* 99). Those successful were Wells and Sgt Sweetman, with one confirmed each, P/O H.L. Thomas with a probable, and Sgt A.S. Kronfeld a damaged. The pilot who failed to return was Sgt A.I. Paget. The action began when Wells advised that Bf109s were attacking from above. Just after they turned to avoid the Germans, he noticed four Bf109s flying slowly towards the section at the same height or slightly below. When the lead German aircraft filled the gunsight, Wells opened fire at the Bf109 which passed under him. He saw pieces coming away and observed hits along the entire top of the fuselage. The Bf109 entered a steep dive and almost hit P/O J.F. Knight's Spitfire flying behind and below. Wells continued to watch the Bf109 dive almost vertically to the ground, the pilot making no apparent attempt to pull out. As for Sweetman, he engaged his target for a short time and managed to turn into it, flying slightly below, and in a full beam attack fired a one and a half second burst at 250 yards. He broke off suddenly and the Bf109 was observed falling away, rolling on its back out of control and going in to a vertical dive.

This performance was repeated during the afternoon three days later en route to Gosnay. Flight Lieutenant Wells was leading the squadron and took off at 14.30. As they crossed the French coast, they sighted a number of Bf109s above that were soon diving to attack the New Zealanders. The Kiwis evaded this initial attack without difficulty. Other attacks developed, however, and soon 485 became split up as dogfights were initiated. Wells and his Number 2 (P/O J.F. Knight) were turning towards some enemy aircraft when he saw tracers hitting Knight from below. An enemy aircraft broke downwards immediately and Knight initially seemed to be unaware he had been hit or of the Glycol leak streaming from his aircraft. Wells ordered him to set course for England at once. However, P/O J.F. Knight had to crash land in France and was taken captive. As Wells turned to protect his wingman's tail, a Bf109 came in to attack him from behind. He closed on this Bf109, firing a two or three second burst with both cannon and machine guns from 200-150 yards. He saw large pieces break off the left wing, including what he thought to be an aileron. Then black smoke began to pour out from underneath. The Bf109 started a downward spiral and Wells saw the pilot bale out a few seconds later. He didn't have time to enjoy his victory as he was set upon by four more Bf109s that delivered a series of well-coordinated attacks as they chased him from east of Boulogne to half way back across the Channel. During these attacks, the Spitfire was hit twice, first by cannon shells, then by machine gun fire. The first pair of 109s approached in line astern, firing as they closed, forcing Wells to turn back to face them, while the second pair had climbed 1000 feet above him into the sun. Each time Wells resumed his course for home, the pair above dived as the original pair repositioned themselves. This happened continually until the wingman of one of the pairs, instead of breaking off behind, overshot and pulled out ahead. Wells seized the opportunity to fire at the Bf109 with everything he had from about 100 yards and saw small bits flying off and copious amounts of black smoke appearing. While the German pilot managed to take evasive action, Wells was able to give him another burst from about the same range. The Bf109 turned over and, in a few seconds, Wells saw the Messerschmitt going steadily down, burning furiously, five miles west of Boulogne. For Wells it was his second double claim after the first made on 5 July flying a Spitfire II. During this combat, two more pilots scored: P/O G.H. Francis claimed a third Bf109 destroyed and P/O W.V. Crawford-Compton added a probable. The rest of the month was uneventful if Sgt W.M. Krebs wrecking a Spitfire during a training flight on the 26th is ignored.

October started well with S/L Knight damaging a Bf109 on the 1st while on a fighter sweep to the Saint-Omer/Le Touquet area, and three 109s were credited as probable to F/L Wells, F/O R.H. Strang and Sgt J.D. Rae on the 2nd while on a fighter patrol over the Dunkirk area and Ostend. The next day, the squadron was airborne again for a Circus, but no combat developed and 485 returned to base without incident. There was something to celebrate, however, as the CO was awarded the DFC. The next few days were quiet and, excluding a shipping reconnaissance carried out by Strang and Rae, no sorties were flown until the 12th when another Circus, with Gravelines as the target, proved to be totally uneventful. Just after lunch on the 13th, the squadron took off for another Circus (No. 108A), a close escort to Arques. Enemy aircraft were encountered off the French coast. Soon after crossing the coast, P/O Crawford-Compton saw a Messerschmitt diving from 12,000 feet to attack Spitfires from the Australian 452 Squadron. He immediately dived on the third aircraft and, just as he got within range, the Bf109 turned away, giving him a fine quarter attack. He fired a short burst and the aircraft straightened out with a thin stream of black smoke coming from the engine. The Bf109 made no attempt at evasive action. Crawford-Compton closed to 50 yards and fired another burst. This proved fatal as the Messerschmitt caught fire and spun down. Its descent was confirmed by P/O H.L. Thomas and Sgt I.J. McNeil and the claim was filed for a confirmed Bf109 destroyed. Another claim was made during this engagement, by P/O L.P. Griffith, for a damaged Bf109. The weather did not permit much flying for several days after with just a fighter sweep to Boulogne by six aircraft flown on the 17th and a convoy patrol the following day. On the 21st, a Rodeo to Saint-Omer was flown in the morning, led by the CO, and many enemy aircraft were encountered, the Kiwis returning with a Bf109 claimed as destroyed (Sgt A.S. Kronfeld) and one damaged (Sgt I.J. McNeill). That would be the last operation from Redhill as, in the afternoon, the squadron moved to Kenley to become part of the Kenley Wing. The first operation from the new base was carried out on the 24th, the wing leader, W/C E.N. Ryder, flying with the Kiwis for the occasion. Two days later, the squadron carried out a Channel patrol for returning fighters, the CO leading. The unit was led by the wing leader again on the 29th for an offensive op over the Channel, but all aircraft returned to base without incident. Two days later, W/C Ryder took off at the head of the squadron to escort Hurricanes to Dunkirk. While many German aircraft were seen, no combat ensued. However, flak was more effective and Ryder was seen to break away from the formation towards France where he was ultimately captured. To balance this loss somewhat, F/L Wells was awarded a Bar to his DFC the same day. With the weather degrading

Spitfire VB BM239/N with F/O J.G. Pattison in the cockpit at Kenley. John Pattison would later command 485 Sqn for his last tour of operations between September 1944 and February 1945. (via P. Sortehaug)

from November, the number of sorties logically decreased with about 100 flown in November and a meagre 65 in December. The number of hours flown on non-operational flights was 293.3 and 423.6 respectively. The first action of November took place on the 6th, under the command of the new wing leader, W/C J.R.A. Peel, with an escort to the Calais/Cap Gris-Nez area. German fighters were spotted over Cap Gris-Nez and dived on the New Zealanders. At the end of the ensuing dogfight, P/O W.V. Crawford-Compton and Sgt J.D. Rae each claimed one Bf109 as probably destroyed. Over the next two days, 485 was airborne to provide escort for Hurricanes attacking Le Tréport on the 7th and to provide high cover to bombers attacking Lille. A sweep followed on the 9th, as did two Ramrods on the 11th and 18th, W/C Peel flying with the squadron each time. On the 23rd, a change of command took place with F/L Wells becoming the new CO. It was W/C Peel, however, who would fly once more with 485 for the last op of November, an escort for Hurricanes to Boulogne Harbour. December mainly consisted of patrols with two Rhubarbs led by F/L R.H. Strang, the B Flight commander from mid-October, breaking the routine. The only offensive op was flown on the 28th, an uneventful fighter sweep to Le Touquet led by S/L Wells. The next day, three Spitfires were operating from Martlesham Heath on patrol, but were unable to locate the shipping they were to protect. Pilot Officer J.J. Palmer, who took off five minutes later for the same patrol, located the convoy and patrolled for about three minutes at 1500/2000 feet without seeing the rest of the section. Forty-five minutes later he saw a Ju88 flying over the convoy at the same height and 600 yards away. He turned to make a quarter astern attack. As he did so, he saw two aircraft above at 5 o'clock and 100 yards apart. He continued towards the Junkers, but was attacked by two Bf109s. Palmer turned away from the bomber and lost all three enemy aircraft in cloud. He was then hit in the engine and wings by cannon shells and gained a little height. The engine finally cut out and Palmer decided to bale out off Harwich from 2000 feet. He climbed into his dinghy uninjured and was fortunate to be rescued by a motor launch.

The first major operation of 1942 was carried out on 6 January with an offensive patrol from Kenley led by the new wing leader, W/C R.F. Boyd. The op was flown at 13,500 feet, but proved uneventful. Until the 25th, operational activity consisted of patrols, but on that day, W/C Boyd, with 485 and the Australians from 452, left Kenley to join the Northolt Wing for a fighter sweep that headed to Le Touquet soon after the rendezvous. Flight Lieutenant R.H. Strang's aircraft inexplicably dived into the sea off Dover from a great height. Oxygen failure was believed to be the cause. Otherwise the mission was uneventful. Strang was replaced by P/O Crawford-Compton at the head of B Flight. January ended with a Rhubarb of four Spitfires led by the CO on the 26th, and another fighter sweep with the Wing the following day, but nothing of interest occurred on either op. In all, less than ninety sorties were flown in January. February was no improvement with less than eighty sorties completed. The weather prevented any flying during the first week of the month, and operations resumed with patrols. On 12 February, the New Zealanders participated in the 'Channel Dash'. The British had been aware of the intention of the German warships *Gneisenau*, *Prinz Eugen* and *Scharnhorst*, moored at Brest, to make a break for Germany via the Channel. On the day in question, 12 February, the squadron was ordered to the scene of the breakout where enemy fighters were encountered in force. The squadron could count not only the wing leader, W/C Boyd, in

A photograph for the press following the squadron's success during the 'Channel Dash' on 12 February 1942. From left to right: H.N. Sweetman, D.T. Clouston, B.E. Gibbs, R.J.C. Grant, M.M. Shand, E.P. Wells, I.J. McNeil, W.V. Crawford-Compton, J.M. Checketts and R.W. Baker. Collectively, these officers would earn four DSOs, eleven DFCs, a DFM and four would command the squadron. *(via P. Sortehaug)*

The King's visit to Kenley at the end of April 1942. Above, the King speaking with F/Sgt A.R. Robson who has just landed following a sweep. Below, the King being introduced to pilots including Flight J.R.C. Kilian with whom he is shaking hands. *(via P. Sortehaug)*

its ranks, but also the station commander, G/C F.V. Beamish. The Wing was tasked with escorting Beauforts, but the latter were not met at Manston as arranged so the Wing proceeded to the target. The German ships were, of course, protected by the Luftwaffe and aerial combat was inevitable. Against no losses, two Bf109s were shot down by Crawford-Compton and P/O RJC. Grant, and another jointly claimed by Pilot Officers D.T. Clouston and H.N. Sweetman, while F/L G.H. Francis claimed a Fw190. In addition, Crawford-Compton damaged another Bf109 while Sergeant J.D. Rae probably destroyed a second. It was a grey day with cloud cover clamped right down and the section led by S/L E.P. Wells failed to connect with enemy aircraft. They therefore amused them-selves by strafing an E-Boat, which was last observed sinking. As a result of these successes the squadron's exploits were lavishly featured in the British media. The Kiwis flew two other major operations over the continent before the end of the month, on the 13th and 26th, but no claims or losses were reported. In March the number of sorties increased markedly with 170 carried out. Furthermore, the beginning of the month started with the celebration of the award of DFCs to F/L W.V. Crawford-Compton and F/L G.H. Francis, the latter having taken over as A Flight commander from Wells in November. He had just left for a rest and his position was assumed by P/O R.J.C. Grant. The main activity of the squadron in March remained escorts. Most were completed without incident, but, on 3 March, No.11 Group's Engineering Officer, W/C Don Finlay, flying with 485 Squadron during a diver-sionary sweep, shot down a Bf109 into the sea off Cap Gris-Nez. Later, on 9 March, while escorting bombers to Mazingarbe, the Wing was engaged while weaving off Le Touquet. Pilot Officer M.R.D. Hume was the only pilot of the squadron to make a claim, a Fw190 probably destroyed. On 26 March 485 participated in a Wing escort to Le Havre. The bombing was successful and on the return journey several enemy aircraft were encountered. In the ensuing engagement, F/L Crawford-Compton fired a four second burst in a diving attack on a Bf109 at 13,000 feet. The Messerschmitt fell away smoking and crashed into the sea 300 yards east of Le Havre. He then shared in the destruction of another with P/O E.D. Mackie and a third was claimed by Sgt I.J.P. Maskill. Pilot Officer W.M. Krebs was shot down off the French coast and, although he baled out, his body was sadly not recovered. Two days later, the Wing, led by G/C F.V. Beamish, took off for a massive fighter patrol to the Cap Gris-Nez/Gravelines area. They made land-fall at Cap Griz-Nez thirty minutes after take-off and some forty to fifty enemy aircraft were seen, rapidly identified as Fw190s accompanied by some Bf109s. They were flying in loose formation between 15,000 and 20,000 feet. Group Captain Beamish turned the Wing sharply to the left to intercept, but individual dogfights ensued almost immediately. The squadron flight commanders scored, with one confirmed victory for F/L W.V. Crawford-Compton and two for F/L R.J.C. Grant (one of which would later be downgraded to probably destroyed). Sergeant J.D. Rae claimed two Fw190s destroyed, but after investigation on return, he was credited with one destroyed and one damaged. Two other pilots made a claim in the course of the combat: P/O G.J. Palmer reported one probably destroyed Fw190 and F/Sgt J.R Liken claimed one Fw190 damaged. The latter was to also be an eyewitness to the loss of the G/C Beamish while being attacked by Fw190s. Liken warned the Kenley Station OC over the radio of the attack, while F/L Grant saw the group captain's aircraft hit under the fuselage and flying slightly nose down soon after. It proceeded out over the coast about five miles ENE of Calais, heading approximately northwest. Flight Lieutenant Grant weaved behind and above to cover him as Beamish's aircraft trailed a little smoke at 13,000 feet. Grant could not complete his job as a Fw190 attacked. He fired his cannons from 150 yards in a left quarter astern attack and saw the Fw190 shudder and continue on its course for a brief period before suddenly blowing up. This was his second success of the day, taking care of another enemy aircraft just before covering G/C Beamish. In the meantime, Crawford-Compton and his section were engaged with three Fw190s. Having positioned astern of the enemy aircraft, the Fw190 on the left turned away as the range was closed. Crawford-Compton followed him, firing a three second burst from 50 yards. He observed hits on the fuselage and wings and then saw the Fw190 turn right over and dive vertically issuing smoke. Crawford-Compton followed the Focke-Wulf from 17,000 feet to 2000 feet when he saw wreckage burning on the ground near Marquise. Pilot Officers R.W. Baker and J.G. Pattison witnessed the attack. The Kiwis did not sustain any loss, so it was a very good day for the squadron even though G/C Beamish failed to return.

April 1942 was a turning point for 485. The Kiwis carried out close to 450 sorties and the many encounters with the Luftwaffe brought a bunch of claims. Three confirmed victories, four probables and five damaged were added to the squadron's tally during the month and most of them resulted from two ops. The first of these claims occurred on the 4th. The Kiwis were flying with the

Spitfire V BM304 arrived at the squadron in April 1942 and would serve throughout the summer.

Kenley, May 1942.
On the wing:
Sgt S.F. Browne (to become the unit's final CO in 1945), Sgt H.R. Leckie (PoW with 152 Sqn in North Africa), P/O P.H. Gaskin, F/Sgt A.R. Robson (PoW 13.02.43), F/O M.G. Barnett, Sgt J.F.P. Yeatman, F/L D.W. Higson (squadron medical officer), P/O D.T. Clouston, F/O K. Hitchins (administration officer), F/L M.M. Shand (PoW 28.11.42), Sgt D.G.E. Brown, and F/O G.R. Miller (squadron adjutant).
Front:
F/O R. Webb (323 Wing Leader in 1944), F/O L.S. Black, F/O D.J. McCready (administration officer), Sgt I.P. Maskill, S/L R.J.C. Grant (OC), G/C R.L. Atcherley (Kenley Station CO), W/C E.P. Wells, (Kenley wing leader), F/L R.W. Baker (†22.02.45 as OC 487 Sqn), F/L R.J.C. Kilian, P/O B.E. Gibbs, F/O J.G. Pattison (later CO), F/L W.V. Crawford-Compton, P/O M.R.D. Hume (later CO), F/L Hunter (administration officer), and F/O D.J.V. Henry.

Kenley Wing to escort twelve Bostons. On the return journey, the bombers were attacked near Saint-Omer from above and below by about forty enemy aircraft. The Kiwis tried to help the bombers, but were stopped by Fw190s. Pilot Officer I.J. McNeil saw one of them attacking a Spitfire and went after it in a 30° diving attack. At 300 yards, he fired a three second burst with cannons and machines guns. McNeil suddenly saw the Focke-Wulf flick over and dive vertically, apparently out of control. Just before he pulled out to re-join the bombers, McNeil saw smoke begin emitting from the engine. However, as he and his wingman had to rejoin the bombers, none of them witnessed the German fighter crash, if it did, so on return it was claimed as probably destroyed. Flight Lieutenant Crawford-Compton and Sgt DG.E. Brown each claimed one Fw190 damaged. During this combat, however, the Germans had a clear advantage over the Kiwis who lost two of their own: Pilot Officers E.F. Chandler and T.T. Fox. Both were killed. One week later 485 was involved in another air combat near Gravelines, but it proved ineffective for each of the opposing forces. The same thing happened on the 16th even though the other squadrons of the Wing, 602 and 457, did score. On the 24th the New Zealanders were very busy, being airborne three times during the day. While the first two ops (10.55 and 13.50) were uneventful, the third one (16.45) was certainly not. The squadron, with the rest of the Kenley Wing, got airborne for *Circus* 133 with S/L Wells leading. They made rendezvous with the Tangmere Wing over Beachy Head and crossed the French coast between Hardelot and Le Touquet before turning south. The first to make contact with the Luftwaffe were the Australians of 457 Squadron. They sighted six Fw190s about 3000 feet below and dived to attack. Shortly after, the controller reported more enemy aircraft coming from Abbeville, approaching the Kiwis at 16,000 feet. They were soon sighted to the left and 1000 feet below. Wells led 485 out of the sun onto the German fighters. The latter were flying in a very tight formation and obviously didn't see the Kiwis coming. They discovered their presence when Wells opened fire on one of the (now identified) Fw190s, when he was at about 300 yards, closing to 200 yards, with both cannons and machine guns. His cannons stopped, but he continued to fire at the German aircraft. No immediate result was noticed until he saw the Fw190 go down slowly, appearing to be barely under control. Shortly after he saw the aircraft turning slowly into a spiral. Wells had time to see it crash in a large ploughed paddock where it disappeared in a mass of flame. In the meantime, other pilots scored. Flight Lieutenant W.V. Crawford-Compton claimed one Fw190 confirmed, while P/O J.J. Palmer and F/L J.R.C. Kilian (flying as supernumerary flight lieutenant) each claimed a probable Fw190. However, Kilian's claim was later downgraded to damaged. These claims were made against no loss from the squadron's ranks. The next day, the CO scored again with a Fw190 damaged near Nieuport during Circus 137. The following day the squadron was airborne twice. In the evening, during a fighter sweep near Calais, 485 Squadron was bounced out of the sun by Fw190s and lost three Spitfires. Flying Officer J.G. Pattison and F/Sgt J.R. Liken both managed to glide across the Channel and baled out into the sea off Dungeness where they were picked up. Liken, however, sadly died of his wounds. Flight Sergeant T.C. Goodlet also used his parachute and was captured. Pilot

Officer Mackie recorded the only success of the day when a Fw190 he had fired a long burst at emitted a cloud of black smoke as it went down near Mardyck. It was only claimed as probably destroyed. The next day P/O J.J. Palmer was shot down by a Focke-Wulf near Armentieres and joined Goodlet in a PoW camp while F/L W.V. Crawford-Compton crashed back at base, sustaining an injury that forced him to leave the unit, temporarily suspended from operations. These two losses were partially balanced by F/Sgt A.R. Robson being credited with probably destroying one of the four Fw190s he fired at. The same pilot scored again two days later with a Fw190 claimed as damaged near Le Touquet.

On 1 May F/Sgt A.R. Robson scored again and damaged a Fw190, but P/O J.R. Falls failed to return. This occurred during an escort of eight Hurri-bombers in conjunction with the West Malling and Northolt Wings. The Kenley Wing was attacked by thirty enemy aircraft, between Marquise and Calais, which forced the Wing to disperse. Falls was hit, evacuated his aircraft near Marquise and was taken prisoner. After an uneventful Rodeo, the Wing, led by S/L Wells, flew a fighter sweep to the Hardelot/Sangatte area on 4 May. The squadron was attacked by about twenty Fw190s around Ambleteuse and, in the ensuing dogfights, F/Sgt A.R. Robson scored again with a Fw190 probably destroyed, as did F/O M.M. Shand, but at the cost of two Spitfires and one pilot: P/O J.M. Checketts and F/Sgt D.M. Russell. Both had to parachute into the Channel from their stricken aircraft, the former being rescued, but the latter sadly dying of exposure. Despite the fact that May, with over 400 sorties completed, was another very busy month, no further claims were made before the start of June. No claims, but losses were suffered as F/L M.G. Barnett and Sgt S.F. Browne failed to return from a combat with Fw190s around Abbeville. They baled out, and eventually evaded capture. Browne was at large for a fortnight until he was taken prisoner by the French at Caussade after getting across the demarcation line. He was interned at Fort de la Revère, an old frontier fort situated at 3000 feet at the top of the mountain range that runs along the coast above Nice and Monte Carlo. Here he was surprised to find Barnett already in residence. Barnett, he learned, had vacated his aircraft at 3000 feet and landed unharmed in a small plantation. Disguising himself to look like a French worker, he succeeded in making his way to Paris by train and, with French assistance, travelled to Bordeaux in a matter of days. Unfortunately, things came unstuck after he reached the small village of Frontenac and he had just crossed the border into unoccupied France when he was arrested. He was handed over to the local Gendarmerie and entrained under escort to Toulouse and then to the mountaintop fort. In mid-August the officers got word that they were about to be moved to another camp so several, Barnett included, made a bid to escape the night before. They filed and broke their way out of the fort and made for Monaco, where they could buy some time as the French police would have to acquire permission from the authorities before they could conduct any sort of search. Here the escapees hid in a flat for several days, until the flap died down, and made for safe houses in Marseille where they were placed in the hands of an underground organisation. After three weeks in Marseille, they were moved individually, but under escort, to Perpignan and then on to the seaside resort of Canet-Plage. Here, the following day, Barnett was re-united with Stan Browne who had taken part in a mass

By the end of 1942 a new generation of pilots had been posted in. From left to right:
Sgt L.S.M. White, P/O G.J. Moorhead (†30.05.43), F/L R.W. Baker (A Flight CO), P/O M.G. Sutherland (PoW 22.08.43, but repatriated in September 1944 with a leg amputated), Sgt C.J. Sheddan (CO 486 Sqn by the end of the war), P/O I.P.J. Maskill (CO 91 Sqn at the end of the war) and Sgt L.B. Gordon (PoW 06.02.43).

Flying Officer D.J.V. Henry posing in front of BM233/OU-E during the summer of 1942. He left the squadron in October to serve in North Africa. Returning to the UK, he served another tour in 1944 with 41 Sqn, but ended the war as a PoW from 10 February 1945. Spitfire BM233 served until 485 received a batch of Mk IX in July 1943. *(via P. Sortehaug)*

escape from the fort, a fortnight after his own. Browne had put up a fine performance by running, without stopping, to Nice, where he was hidden and taken under the wing of the same underground movement that had looked after Barnett. Thereafter, the movements of the pair were similar and they were taken by boat to Gibraltar, and then to England. Both subsequently re-joined the squadron and were welcomed back with great pride and celebration.

The day after Barnett and Browne were shot down, a major change took place with S/L Wells, promoted to wing leader of the Kenley Wing, relinquishing command to F/L R.J.C. Grant, the A Flight commander. The intense rhythm of operations continued in June until the 11th inclusive. The major task remained escorts with eight Circus ops carried out during that period of time. The busiest day was the 4th with two Circuses performed (Nos. 185 and 186), in addition to patrols, making a grand total of 36 sorties. However, despite this intensity, the Kiwis didn't increase their score, but, on the other hand, they didn't suffer any losses. Between the 15th and 21st, 485 was sent to Ipswich, returning to Kenley on the 22nd. They resumed operations in the evening with patrols over the Beachy Head/Hastings zone. More patrols were flown until the end of June. As for offensive operations, escort duties resumed four days later with a Circus, followed by a second on the 29th, led by W/C Wells this time. The two ops were uneventful. The squadron remained at Kenley until 8 July when it was withdrawn to Kingscliffe, east of Leicester, for a rest where it was engaged in aerodrome defence, convoy patrols off the Norfolk coast, and Rhubarbs over Belgium and Holland. While the number of operations steadily dropped, with 140 sorties achieved in July, Rhubarbs remained dangerous and unfortunately resulted in three pilots reported missing in the space of a fortnight for little tangible reward. Pilot Officer H.W. Harrison, an Englishman, disappeared on 22 July, Sgt N.M. Langlands on 2 August, and Sgt R.W. Vessey on the 3rd. Vessey's loss was somewhat balanced by the New Zealanders making a claim. Blue section, consisting of P/O I.P.J. Maskill and F/O L.S. Black, took off at 17.30 from Decking and flew to Wittering to orbit. After various vectors and indications of bandits, and after seeing bomb bursts on Wellingborough, Black saw an enemy aircraft at 18.12. Getting into position behind and to the right, he fired a six second burst with cannons and machine guns from about 400 yards. The enemy aircraft, identified as a Do217, climbed into cloud where it disappeared, but Black followed it and made contact again. He got into a good position from above and behind and gave two short bursts with machine guns at 100 yards. At this range he was also in range of the German gunners and experienced inaccurate return fire, but it forced him to turn away. That was enough for the Dornier which entered a dive. When Black came out of cloud he saw the Do217 blazing on the ground. However, in the same period of time, 485 lost another Spitfire in an accident when BP858, flown by P/O B.E. Gibbs, was damaged in a formation landing when it collided with BM522 at Kingscliffe. Gibbs' aircraft was too damaged to repair and was struck off charge a week later. The most significant event to occur during this period was the Dieppe raid on 19 August 1942, with 485 Squadron providing a maximum effort for the operation. Forty-four sorties were flown that day, roughly a quarter of the entire operational activity for the month. During the course of the day, the unit supplied aircraft on four occasions with W/C P.G. Jameson, a New Zealander and the Wittering wing leader, as well as P/O C. Chrystall, setting fire to Fw190s. The latter got his Fw190 by attacking from the stern quarter at about 100 yards with a 2-3 second burst. He then broke sharply to the left and turned to see the Fw190 going down and the pilot baling out. Two other claims were also made. Pilot Officer L.S. Black damaged another Fw190 and F/L R.W. Baker damaged a Do217. The rest of the month was rather quiet and, excluding escorts performed on the 20th and the 29th, operational activity consisted of patrols. On 1 September, Sgt R.D. Riley was lost during a Rhubarb. He was last seen after attacking barges on a canal running from Haarlem. Soon after, he was heard saying he had been hit. He was later reported as a prisoner of the Germans. The remainder of September and October proved quiet with little activity recorded over about 100 and sixty sorties respectively. No further losses or claims were recorded during this period, but the squadron did not operate over the continent consistently. It spent a while in Northern Ireland early in November, returning to Kingscliffe in the middle of the month. A few sorties were flown before the end of month. On the 23rd, a Rhubarb was flown from Martlesham, with F/L J.G. Pattison in the lead, the target being railways and canals in Belgium and Holland. This was followed by another Rhubarb three days later, this time led by P/O A.R. Robson, from Coltishall and was also completed without incident. On the 28th, the CO, with four other pilots, flew down to Martlesham where they took off to attack shipping on the Zuid-Beveland Canal. Squadron Leader Grant left the four other pilots shortly after reaching the Dutch coast and flew south to Sehouwen, near Zierikzee, where he met light flak that forced him to change course. That was a good thing as he immediately saw a He115 straight ahead at 300 feet. He pulled up and opened fire with cannons and machine guns from about 250 yards below and dead astern. He observed strikes on the floats and under the wings. He fired a second burst from about 150 yards, again from dead astern, and saw the left engine catch fire. The seaplane dived into the sea soon after. In the meantime, the four other Spitfires continued their sortie and P/O Black and Sgt F.W. Norris attacked an oil barge then climbed into cloud and set course for home. Only Black made it, Sgt Norris was posted missing. The pair consisting of F/L M.M. Shand and Sgt H.S. Tucker was not much luckier. They attacked a train near Goes and climbed to 800 feet where they were attacked by Fw190s. Tucker saw his tailplane, mainplane and radio hit, but managed to escape and return to England. Shand was also hit and eventually shot down to become a prisoner of war. His OC B Flight position was taken over by F/L Pattison the next day. Shand later achieved notoriety by taking part in the mass escape from Sagan, being the second last prisoner out of the tunnel, but was recaptured and fortunately spared the executions that followed. The squadron flew 65 sorties in December, but nothing changed until it moved to Westhampnett on 2 January 1943, rejoining 11 Group to return to frontline operations. This station was part of the Tangmere Sector. The next day, 485 went into action again with 26 sorties carried out, a Circus in the morning (No. 247) and a Rodeo in the afternoon (No. 142). Even though the weather was not very favourable in January, the New Zealanders flew more than 250 sorties. The squadron flew with the wing leader, W/C P.M. Brothers, on occasion and had various encounters with the Luftwaffe, particularly on the 21st near Abbeville during as escort and on the 26th near Hardelot, during which Brothers claimed a Fw190 destroyed. February could be divided in two. During the first half, 100 sorties were flown, with five major operations, three Rodeos (2nd, 3rd and 13th), one Rhubarb (6th), and one Circus (10th). As far as 485 was concerned, the first two Rodeos and the Circus were uneventful, but the single Rhubarb was completed for the cost of P/O L.B. Gordon who became a prisoner after attacking a train near Néville. On the 13th, S/L Grant led 485 and 610 Squadrons over Northern France, the original idea being to engage a standing patrol over Boulogne that was guarding an enemy vessel in the harbour. The Wing was at 20,000 feet, when it crossed on the way in at Hardelot, and swept north as far as Desvres. At 12.15 the Wing was engaged in the Hardelot area and numerous dogfights ensued. Grant claimed a Fw190 destroyed, after a dangerous head-on attack from about 10° to the left, with cannons and machine guns at a range of approximately 250 yards. He had to turn quickly to avoid a collision and the Fw190 shot past him with black smoke pouring from the engine. After climbing above him, the German fighter flicked on to its back and went down in a tight spin before crashing about six miles inland of Hardelot. Another pilot, F/O M.R.D. Hume, claimed a second Fw190 destroyed while F/O D.G.E.

A side view of Spitfire BM247/OU-T in which Sgt N.M. Langlands was lost on 2 August 1942

With five pilots escaping from France and another evading capture during the unit's existence, it is thought that the squadron set a record for 'home runs' for a fighter unit in WW2. Here M.G. Barnett (left) and S.F. Browne (right) are talking to each other after their return to Great Britain in the autumn of 1942. *(via P. Sortehaug)*

Brown claimed another as damaged. The Germans, however, had success as three of 485's pilots failed to return: F/O I.A.C. Grant and Sgt R.J. Steed were both killed while F/O A.R. Robson became a PoW. Flying Officer Grant was the commanding officer's brother, making this loss particularly painful for the CO. Two days later, the squadron suspended operations as it was sent on an air firing course at Martlesham Heath, returning to Westhampnett on 7 March. Operations resumed under the leadership of S/L Grant for a short time as a new CO was appointed on the 20th. Squadron Leader R.W. Baker had been leading A Flight for the past ten months. His position was taken over by P/O M.R.D. Hume. During the month, excluding a handful of Rodeos, the New Zealanders were mostly employed flying patrols. March was free of losses, but no claims were made either. The first week of April was highlighted by two big operations, one Rodeo on the 3rd involving the Tangmere Wing (485 and 610 Sqns), and, the following day, an escort for Venturas attacking Caen aerodrome. In both cases, aerial combat took place, but no claim was made. However, the squadron lost one pilot on 4 April when Sgt H.J. Oxley was shot down and killed by Fw190s. The Kiwis returned over the continent a week later on the 13th to escort Venturas attacking the marshalling yards at Caen. The bombers dropped their loads and, soon after, the formation was attacked by eight Fw190s. The New Zealanders were flying as close escort to the rear six bombers and Sgt T.W.J. Denholm became another victim of the Fw190s. Over the following days, 485 continued to be very active in the escort role over the continent. The next four escorts were carried out without incident, but, on the 21st, a furious combat took place between the New Zealanders and Fw190s, that tried to intercept the Venturas the squadron was escorting, west of Cayeux. Sergeant G.H. Meagher was flying close to the Venturas when he saw two Bf109s approaching from 4 o'clock. One had time to attack a Ventura, setting an engine on fire. The Bf109 then climbed in front of Meagher in order to make another pass on the bomber. Meagher attacked it from 45 degrees astern and fired one burst at a range of 50-60 yards. The German hung for a moment and then dived straight down, Meagher watching it crash into the sea. The Bf109 was credited as destroyed. That would be the last offensive operation for the month, the squadron not even flying operationally until the 28th, when an uneventful scramble was ordered, followed by convoy patrols the next day. In April 485 flew close to 300 sorties, but this figure was exceeded in May with 335 sorties performed. The squadron remained active over the continent, operating from Merston near Portsmouth from 21 May onwards, but no substantial encounters with the Luftwaffe occurred and no claims were made. While no losses were recorded during this type of ops, one pilot was lost during a weather reconnaissance on 30 May. Returning from the Cherbourg/Fécamp area at very low altitude, F/O G.J. Morehead hit the sea with the tip of his propeller about 15 miles from the English coast. He climbed to 1000 feet, as if he was attempting to bale out, but then lost height after apparently deciding to ditch. The aircraft stalled just above the water's surface and dropped a wing into the sea. Flying Officer M.G. Sutherland, his wingman, circled the position to obtain a fix, but nothing could be seen. The subsequent ASR mission didn't find anything either. Operations continued in June until the 13th. On the 10th, while escorting Mitchells to bomb Ghent power station, the formation was attacked by Fw190s. Flight Lieutenant M.R.D. Hume and F/Sgt L.S.M. White were in a good position to fire at one of the attackers and claimed it as damaged. That was the only claim made by the Kiwis who sustained no loss. While nobody knew it yet, it was to be the last claim the squadron made while equipped with the Spitfire V. During the last fortnight of June, the unit was practically stood down and no ops were flown. A number of the pilots were sent to Ayr in Scotland where they were required to practice take-offs and landings on the aircraft carrier HMS *Argus*. The other pilots remained at Merston on readiness, but nothing of note occurred. By the end of June, all was back to normal. By that time, 485 had the following Spitfire Mk.Vs on charge: AR493, BL956, BM117/S, BM147, BM200/P, BM203/M, BM233/E, BM238/C, BM323/L, BM353, BM459/R, BM509, BM516/U, BM539/J, EP183/T, EP185, EP387/N, EP277/H and EP767.

At the beginning of July 1943, No. 485 Squadron moved to Biggin Hill to replace No. 611 Squadron as the latter moved out for a rest away from the front line. The latter unit left its Spitfire Mk.IXs behind, resulting in an equipment upgrade that was a huge morale boost for 485; at the same time, it received a new commanding officer, F/L 'Johnny' Checketts transferring from 611 to replace a tour-expired S/L Baker. Checketts had previously served with 485 Squadron during 1942, when he had been shot down. Biggin Hill was Fighter Command's premier station and the cream of its leaders were based there. Group Captain 'Sailor' Malan, a South African, was station commander and W/C Al Deere, a New Zealander like Checketts, was wing leader. While stationed at Biggin Hill, 485's predominant duties were fighter sweeps and escorting bombers attacking targets in France, activities that were to attract plenty of air opposition. During the month, three USAAF officers – Major J.R. Haun, Captain J.R. Walker and Lieutenant E.B. Travis – were attached to the squadron to gain tactical experience in flying Spitfires on offensive operations. On the 14th, while providing cover for returning Fortresses, W/C Deere, who was flying with 485, claimed a probable Fw190 which he last saw making for the French coast streaming smoke. Squadron Leader Checketts damaged another but Captain Walker, one of the Americans, failed to return. In the vicinity of Bernay, a Mk.IX was seen in a shallow dive, trailing smoke from its port radiator, the victim of an attack by a single Fw190; this was presumed to have been Walker. The following afternoon, while providing top cover for Bostons attacking Poix, the squadron was jumped by about 15–20 Fw190s over Crécy Forest. Checketts initially asked for assistance from No. 341 (Free French) Squadron, another Biggin Hill Wing unit, but 485 managed to avoid the first attack. Checketts soon took advantage of the situation and managed to get a shot at one of the attackers from 300 yards astern. He closed to 100 yards and saw strikes on the left mainplane close to the fuselage. He continued firing and suddenly the Fw190 rolled slowly over on its back and went straight down with flames streaming from its belly; the Fw190 was credited as destroyed. Meanwhile, F/O 'Jack' Rae got one more and a probable, and P/O H.S. Tucker got another probable, but the New Zealanders returned home with one of their own missing; F/Sgt T.S.F. Kearins had been shot down in flames by the Fw190s. Kearins, to everyone's surprise, not only survived the ordeal but, with the aid of the French, was able to get back to England later in the year. More cover sorties were carried out during the last fortnight of July and further claims were made. A high-cover escort for Marauders attacking Tocqueville during the evening of the 27th saw the squadron destroy four Fw190s for no loss. Squadron Leader Checketts shot down two in flames and damaged another, while F/Sgt W.T.H. Strahan got a third. Flying Officer Rae damaged a fourth in a high-speed vertical dive before running out of ammunition. He called upon his wingman, P/O Tucker, to finish it off, which he did after the German pilot levelled out. The claim was shared by the two pilots. The following morning, Checketts damaged a Bf109 in the vicinity of Amsterdam and, in the evening of the last day of July, he chased another from 20,000 feet all the way down to ground-level before seeing it crash into a barn in an orchard near Trouville. On the same operation, F/O B.E. Gibbs damaged an Fw190. Definitively, the CO was the man of

In July 1943, 485 began to fly the Mk IX which was able to challenge the Fw190. Here JK762/OU-W which was lost on 20 October with FL R.L. Baker. Note the absence of any visible serial.

the month with six claims to his credit. In August, 485 continued to score and a dozen claims were made across 330 sorties. The series started on the 4th when F/L M.G. Barnett damaged an Fw190, but the highlight in the squadron's history occurred during a Circus to Saint-Omer on the evening of 9 August. A section of four Spitfires bounced eight Bf109s at 10,000 feet in the vicinity of Lille–Merville. In an engagement lasting barely 60 seconds, Checketts claimed three destroyed and probably a fourth, while Flying Officers Rae and Gibbs, and Pilot Officer Tucker, each claimed one destroyed. Among the top-scoring pilots of the moment was 'Jack' Rae who, after having done well over Malta, was continuing to perform over the Continent. On the 17th, he celebrated his recent promotion to flight lieutenant by downing two Bf109s in a most impressive fashion. The squadron was returning from a bomber escort when he spied the pair about to attack a formation of Spitfires, south of Desvres. Rae led his section in, shooting down the leader in a head-on attack, before turning and, after a brief dogfight, downing the wingman. Shortly before midday two days later, south of Abbeville, F/L M.R.D. Hume attacked a Bf109 which blew up, while Checketts and Flying Officers Tucker and M.G. Sutherland damaged three others. So far, 485 had been able to enhance its scoreboard without sustaining any loss but the winds of change blew on the 22nd, a day that proved to be the bleakest in the squadron's history as it was badly mauled while providing high cover for Marauders bombing Beaumont-le-Roger. It was late afternoon when, 10 miles east of Le Havre en route to the target, the New Zealanders met two squadrons of enemy aircraft head on and at identical height. Flying Officer Rae shot down an Fw190 and then experienced engine trouble, forcing him to land close to the French coast, where he was taken prisoner, putting a stop to his ascendancy. He was a huge loss to the squadron as, with the victories he had claimed during the Siege of Malta, he had increased his score to 13 confirmed. Other pilots were also posted missing: P/O L.S.M. White's engine was shot up by a number of Fw190s, but he also managed to destroy one of his attackers before force landing in an open field south-west of Fauville. A pair of Fw190s circled the downed Spitfire but did not fire; White ran off at the appearance of some German troops. During the days following, he was taken in by a succession of French sympathisers, fed and, by entraining and cycling through Paris, Bourges, Marmagne, Reuilly and Toulouse, was able to obtain serious help at Pezens. There, his passage to freedom across the Pyrenees into Spain was initiated and, by 5 October, he was back in England. It was a classic escape made even more remarkable by the fact White had little knowledge of French. Flying Officer Sutherland and P/O Fraser Clark were also shot down, the former baling out with severe wounds and the latter being killed. Sutherland, a big man, had taken a cannon shell through his right leg, fainted but regained consciousness long enough to bale out. He fainted again and came around to find himself on the ground surrounded by enemy soldiers who rushed him to a hospital. There, doctors and nurses tended to him for three weeks until a decision was made to amputate the leg. Early in the new year, he was relocated to Stalag Luft III until shortly after D-Day when he was repatriated. Despite this severe blow, the Kiwis were airborne every day but the 28th and 29th. One more enemy aircraft was shot down during that period, this being a Fw190 near Armentières by P/O John A Houlton on the 27th. There was more bad news in store on 6 September, though, when the commanding officer was shot down in flames on an evening escort to Serqueux. In the vicinity of the target, a large gaggle of Focke-Wulfs and Messerschmitts appeared and, in the melee that followed, Checketts shot one down, probably another, and damaged a third, while F/L Ken C Lee damaged another. Checketts was then shot down, having to exit his burning Spitfire east of Cayeux, with the Fw190 responsible circling him. He landed in a field burned and wounded, hid his parachute and was taken to a safe house by a Frenchman, where his injuries were treated. At one point, his face swelled so badly he could not see.

After about a month, he was moved to Auxi-le-Château where he received the surprise of his life when, among a group of airmen, he recognised the familiar face of Terry Kearins, who had been shot down two months earlier and given up for dead. Like Checketts, he had parachuted from his flaming Spitfire and landed on the Mouriez plateau with severe burns to his legs. With the assistance of a young boy, and despite his pain, he hid in a wood while Germans searched for him close by. He was eventually hidden by a French couple close to the little village of Zeauvise, near Le Quesnoy-en-Artois, who tended his wounds for more than two months, before being handed over to the Resistance network. Following their reunion, Checketts and Kearins travelled in tandem, boarded a train for Paris and later took the Brest–Paris express to Vannes. The next hop took them to Quimper, then Crozon, and lastly to Camarat, a small fishing village at the entrance to Brest Harbour. None of these moves were straight-

Of Māori parentage, Bert Wipiti joined the RNZAF in January 1941. He completed his training in New Zealand and sailed for Singapore in July, becoming the first Māori airman to serve overseas. Posted to No. 243 Squadron as an NCO, he converted to the Brewster Buffalo, a type that had just become operational when the Japanese attacked Malaya in December. He opened his score on 10 January 1942 when he shared in the destruction of a Ki-46. Four more claims followed during the month. At the end of January, 243 was disbanded and merged with No. 453 (RAAF) Squadron with which Wipiti continued to struggle against the Japanese who were already overwhelming the British forces. He was finally evacuated to Java, then to India where he arrived in March 1942 having received the DFM. Posted to No. 67 Squadron, he was subsequently posted out at the end of the year and sent to the UK.
After a period of rest and a refresher course, Wipiti joined No. 485 (NZ) Squadron in August 1943. On 16 September, he continued his success by sharing in the destruction of an Fw190. Another shared victory over an Fw190 was added on 3 October to bring his total to seven confirmed victories (three shared). However, on the day he made his last claim, he was shot down over the Somme estuary and posted missing.

forward affairs but fraught with danger. The enemy was always in close proximity and, frequently, premises housing airmen were searched, resulting in urgent evacuations. It was from Camarat that the two were smuggled out to the open sea and freedom aboard a launch; they still could have failed even at that final hurdle. German sailors searched the vessel before it put to sea but were unable to check the hold because of a conglomeration of ropes stacked there. Checketts was able to continue his combat career, that saw him promoted to wing commander, and finish the war.

The new commanding officer was chosen in house, F/L Hume being promoted to the position. On 16 September, while providing high cover for Marauders bombing Beaumont-le-Roger airfield, a mix of Fw190s and Bf109s were sighted attempting to attack the bombers from below and were subsequently engaged. During a tail chase from 22,000 feet right down to ground level, a Bf109 was shot down through the combined efforts of P/O Houlton and W/O B.S. Wipiti, with Houlton damaging a second. A Bf109 was claimed destroyed on the way home by F/L Gibbs. Flying Officer M Metcalfe shot down an Fw190 in flames but was then killed in similar circumstances when another Fw190 got the jump on him. The squadron lost another pilot to undetermined circumstances on the 24th when F/O J.A. Ainge disappeared in the Saint-Valery region. In October, the number of sorties was markedly down on the previous month – 156 against 415 in September. One day was important in October, the 3rd. During the afternoon, while providing withdrawal cover for Bostons returning from Distré, the New Zealanders engaged four Fw190s in the vicinity of Cayeux. Flight Sergeant G.C. Couper and W/O Wipiti shared in shooting one down before another attacked the latter, who did not return. Wipiti was a Taranaki Māori who had valiantly flown Brewster Buffaloes in the defence of Singapore. He had avoided capture by the skin of his teeth, evacuating the city shortly before it fell, and had also survived the sinking of the ship which had made the escape possible. He had an accumulated score of some six victories, at least four of which were Japanese. Other Fw190s engaged and F/O J.E. Mortimer became embroiled with two, both of which he hit, one being credited as a probable and the other damaged. After a head-on exchange with the second, his Spitfire suffered severe damage and a forlorn attempt to get home saw him forced to ditch in the Channel not far from the Somme estuary. It was hardly the perfect dunking as he went in with his straps loose, smacked his head and, in a daze, sank to the seabed with his aircraft. He managed to struggle free, surface and climb into his dinghy. He paddled towards England, but the tide was against him and, next morning, shortly before daybreak, he gingerly floated up the estuary, negotiating a number of enemy sentries en route. After getting ashore and making contact with sympathisers, Mortimer was hidden in safe houses and, following a mixture of adventures, avoided capture. He was reported safe the following September after

Large view of 485 Squadron with the new Spitfire Mk IXs of the second batch in the spring of 1944. Visible on this photo, MK347/P, MK249/J, MK293/A, MJ502/L, MK198/H, MK246/M, MK202/S, MK204/Y.
(via P. Sortehaug)

American forces liberated the village he was hiding in. A third Spitfire went into the sea south of Dungeness after F/Sgt N.E. Frehner experienced engine failure and baled out.

The squadron moved to Hornchurch on the 18th; three other Fw190s were damaged during the remainder of October but at the cost of two fine pilots and three Spitfires. On the 18th, F/L Lee and F/O J.G. Thomson each damaged a Fw190 and, two days later, F/L P.H. Gaskin damaged the third. The losses occurred on 20 October when four Fw190s caught a section from 485 unawares southwest of Ostend. Flying Officers R.L. Baker and Thomson, both very experienced, were killed while F/Sgt F Transom was able to coax his damaged Spitfire back to the English coast where he baled out. The following month, the squadron was sent north to Drem in Scotland for a well-deserved rest, after more than 1,200 sorties carried out in four months, and returned to the Spitfire Mk.V. The older Spitfires were sufficient for ops assigned to recuperating fighter squadrons relatively removed from the front line. In Scotland, only a few sorties were carried out, 20 in all, mostly consisting of scrambles, but punctuated by a few shipping patrols. Training was the daily task for the Kiwis and this period was uneventful apart from the crash of F/O J.G. Dasent on 22 December 1943 during a co-operation exercise with the navy. That morning, the unit's aircraft were making dummy attacks on ships to allow the anti-aircraft gunners to practice training their weapons on fast, and close, attacking aircraft. The Spitfire flown by Dasent failed to recover sufficiently from a low-level pass and its propeller struck the water, disabling the engine. The pilot was able to use his surplus energy to pull up to about 1,000 feet before he baled out. He was reported to clear the aircraft at about 500 feet, but his parachute did not deploy fully and he was found dead when a ship reached him a short while later. Dasent's death was a sad note on which to end the squadron's association with the Spitfire V. At the end of February 1944, 485 Squadron was sent south to be incorporated into 2TAF and the New Zealanders returned to Hornchurch as part of No. 135 Wing, Squadron Leader J.B. Niven, a Scotsman, assuming command from the 21st. He was the only non-Kiwi to lead the squadron. For a few days during March, 485 moved to Llanbedr in Wales where it undertook bombing and air-gunnery instruction with the gyroscopic gunsight, an innovation which virtually eliminated the bad marksman. It was while flying back to Hornchurch in an Auster on the 27th that F/O T.R.D. Kebbell and P/O M. .C Mayston struck bother when, for no apparent reason, their engine failed over rugged Welsh countryside. The Auster nose-dived into the deck from about 200 feet and, while both were fortunate to survive, they were admitted to hospital with severe injuries. During April, 485 began the first of several hops between Advanced Landing Grounds in Sussex, accommodated under canvas (a portent of things to come on the Continent). While operational activity remained low in March and April, with 117 and 195 sorties flown respectively, about 360 were flown in May in the lead up to D-Day. Escorting bombers was the order of the day, and, but for a brief interlude following D-Day, enemy aircraft were seldom sighted.

During the invasion period, the Kiwis were primarily involved in low cover of the landing beaches and adjoining regions, taking off from Selsey near Portsmouth. Their first successes occurred during the afternoon of D-Day itself when F/O Houlton shot down a Ju88 over *Omaha* beach and collaborated with F/L K.J. Macdonald, F/O Mayston and F/Sgt E.G. Atkins to shoot down another.

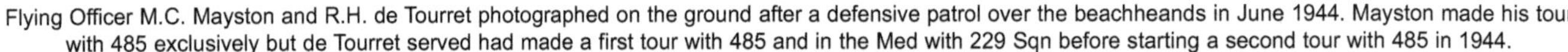

Flying Officer M.C. Mayston and R.H. de Tourret photographed on the ground after a defensive patrol over the beachheands in June 1944. Mayston made his tour with 485 exclusively but de Tourret served had made a first tour with 485 and in the Med with 229 Sqn before starting a second tour with 485 in 1944.

Spitfire ML407/OU-V seen during a patrol during the summer 1944, regularly flown by F/O Houlton on which he made his final claims on 12 June. *(via P. Sortehaug)*

Two days later, F/O J.F.P. Yeatman and Flight Sergeant M.H. Eyre got a Fw190 fighter-bomber attempting to bomb shipping off beaches in the early light. Later that evening, while covering the same beach, the squadron intercepted 12 Bf109s north of Caen with three falling to Flying Officers Houlton and Transom, and P/O H.W.B. Patterson. During the same patrol, F/O A.B. Stead claimed an Fw190 destroyed, while Squadron Leader Niven and W/O H.M. Esdaile each damaged another. Then, just after dawn on 12 June, Flight Lieutenants Houlton and W.A. Newenham shot down two more Bf109s south of Utah beach. On 29 June, Houlton was leading a section at 9,000 feet around Caen when, 15 miles south of the town, 12 Fw190s passed over him at 10,000 feet, flying south. He broke in behind these enemy aircraft which pulled up into cloud, except one straggler which took violent evasive action. Houlton fired several short bursts from 300–200 yards and varying angles astern; he observed strikes on the right wing root and the fuselage. However, Houlton could not go on with the attack, as the enemy fighter entered cloud, so he claimed a damaged. While Houlton would score again while serving with No 274 Squadron in May 1945, he had made 485's final squadron-member claim of the war. Indeed, the fortunes of war would not permit the squadron to add further enemy aircraft to its tally. These successes were accomplished without loss over 650 sorties but, despite this more than satisfying month, it was tainted with an incident on the 10th that saw a squadron pilot shoot down a Royal Navy Seafire. The pilot in question, F/O Stead, was forced to defend himself during a tragic incident of misidentification; a Seafire persistently attacked him, forcing him to shoot it down. The subsequent court of inquiry ruled in Stead's favour and he was exempted from any blame. In July, the number of sorties was cut by half, but no losses were recorded. For most of the month, the squadron was based at Funtington, still close to Portsmouth.

In August, 485 moved to Tangmere on the 19th then to B.17/Caen–Carpiquet in France at the end of the month. Despite those moves, the squadron managed to carry out 370 sorties. The rapid advance of the Allied troops obliged 2TAF to follow and the squadrons became familiar with several moves in quick succession. Therefore, 485 moved to B.35/Le Tréport on the 7th and B.53/Merville on the 12th. It was at the latter a change of command took place mid-month, S/L J Pattison replacing S/L Niven. Pattison had had a chequered career, having been shot down twice, once during the Battle of Britain and once during 1942, but he had redressed the balance by destroying two fighters with No. 66 Squadron shortly before his posting to 485. In October, the front became more stable, so 485 remained at Merville but, on 2 November, settled at B.65/Maldegem in Belgium. Three days later, it attended a gunnery course at Fairwood Common in Wales, during which one Kiwi was killed on the 15th; during an exercise, P/O C.M. McInnes crashed into Swansea Bay. This Armament Practice Camp was important as the Kiwis trained to drop bombs from their Spitfire Mk.IXs.

The move back to Maldegem on 25 November heralded a change in focus with the squadron thereafter assuming more of a fighter-bomber ground attack role, supporting troops and striking at trains, motor transport and gun positions in north-west France, Belgium and Holland with 500 pounders. It was while operating from Belgium that the unit's final claim against an enemy piloted aircraft was made, but it was not made by a squadron member. On Boxing Day, a pair of Me262s were sighted near Stavelot and Wing Commander Ray Harries (wing leader 135 Wing), who was leading 485 on this occasion, engaged and scored strikes on one of the jets.

Pilots of 485 Squadron converting to Tempests, Predannack, Cornwall early 1945. Due to a shortage of aircraft less than a hundred hours was all that could be flown, and most of this was accumulated on Typhoons.
Back row : W/O W.A. Hoskins, W/O M.J.C. Lind, F/O A. Roberts, F/O C.T. Wilton, F/O M.C. Mayston, F/O L. Jordon (Admin), P/O R.M. Clarke, F/O W. Parker (Engineering), W/O M.A. Collett, F/O J. Marsden (Engineering), J. Darragh.
Centre row : W/O H.M. Esdaille, F/O D.L. Iggo, F/L J.N. King, F/L O.L. Hardy, S/L K.J. Macdonald (CO), F/L S.F. Browne, F/L L.M. Ralph, F/L E. Te K Bennett, W/O G. Henderson.
Front : F/O G.C. Earl, F/Sgt O.O. Hunter, F/Sgt A.J. Greer, W/O P.J. Donnelly, F/Sgt P.T. Humphrey. *(via P. Sortehaug)*

The year 1945 opened with the Luftwaffe's all-out attack – Operation *Bodenplatte* – on front-line Allied airfields; the New Zealand squadron was one of the most affected. Six Bf109s hit Maldegem airfield, destroying 11 of the parked Spitfires. Fortunately, there were no fatalities and replacement aircraft were flown in the next day, allowing operations to resume at once. On 6 January, two Spitfires flown by F/L Stead and P/O F.C. Matthews received serious damage when a train they attacked in Holland exploded beneath them. Both pilots succeeded in coaxing their aircraft back behind Allied lines but were killed attempting to crash land. Stead in particular was a big loss as he had fashioned a reputation for being a reliable type and had only just been rewarded with a flight commander's post. Those were the only losses 485 reported on operations for January over 180 sorties. In February, over 220 sorties were performed but for the cost of one pilot; on the 8th, F/O D.G.L. Taylor was killed after striking a lamppost while strafing another train. To summarise, 485 Squadron negotiated the final 18 months of the war with just three combat fatalities (and a further two classified as non-operational). During the same month, on the 21st, F/L K.C. Macdonald, from No. 222 Squadron, became commanding officer, taking the squadron at short notice to Predannack in Cornwall to re-equip with Hawker Tempests. Macdonald was a very experienced pilot, having initially served as a flying instructor back in New Zealand before completing a tour of operations in the Solomon Islands on Kittyhawks. This was his second posting to the squadron, having joined it earlier in the year before taking up a flight commander's post with 222. His experience flying Tempests with that unit made him the best candidate to replace S/L Pattison although a shortage of the type put paid to the plan to re-equip and only a few hours were flown on the new aircraft. At the end of April, after seven weeks of precious little flying on Tempests, the decision was made that the squadron should return to the Continent where it would take possession of some Spitfire Mk.IXBs. As part of No. 132 Wing, at Twente in Holland, and then No. 145 Wing, at Drope in Germany, 485 flew armed recces for the final fortnight of the war, totalling over 100 sorties. It was from Drope on 7 May that the last operation, a patrol over Oldenburg by 12 aircraft, was flown. Shortly after, the unit received a consignment of Spitfire Mk.XVIs, exchanging its aircraft with those of No. 74 Squadron, which had been recalled to the UK. Although hostilities had concluded, flying continued and accidents, as they do, did occur. On 23 June, F/L Jim George was a passenger in a Mosquito of No. 409 (RCAF) Squadron which crashed shortly after take-off from Twente. All on board were killed as were two Dutch civilians. In July, the squadron moved to Fassberg and S/L SF Browne became its final CO. For Browne, this was a defining moment for he had joined the unit as a sergeant pilot in 1942 and in his wildest imagination could hardly have considered eventually leading it. It was he who had the job of winding up the squadron which eventually disbanded on 26 August 1945.

The New Zealanders of 485 Sqn were soon allowed to apply more colourful markings to their Spitfire XVIs. TB675/OU-V is naturally adorned with the silver fern. (*via P. Sortehaug*).

Spitfire XVI OU-T was Squadron Leader K.J. Macdonald's aircraft and was TB622. All seem wearing an insignia ahead the cockpit, a silver fern in a black badge. (*via P. Sortehaug*)

Date	Pilot	SN	Origin	Type	Serial	Code	Nb	Cat.
			SPITFIRE MK II					
02.06.41	S/L Marcus W.B. **KNIGHT**	RAF No. 37408	(NZ)/RAF	Bf109	**P7773**	OU-D	1.0	C
05.07.41	F/L Edward P. **WELLS**	NZ39950	RNZAF	Bf109	**P8022**	OU-Y	2.0	C
08.07.41	P/O Charles **STEWART**	RAF No. 44231	(NZ)/RAF	Bf109	**P7822**	OU-A	1.0	C
24.07.41	F/L Edward P. **WELLS**	NZ39950	RNZAF	Bf109	**P8022**	OU-Y	1.0	C
16.08.41	Sgt Lindsay J. **FRECKLINGTON**	NZ401261	RNZAF	Bf109	**P7438**	OU-Q	1.0	P
19.08.41	Sgt John D. **RAE**	NZ402896	RNZAF	Bf109	**P7621**	OU-Y	1.0	C
			SPITFIRE MK V					
19.08.41	F/L Edward P. **WELLS**	NZ39950	RNZAF	Bf109	**W3406**	OU-H	1.0	C
29.08.41	F/L Stanley C. **NORRIS**	RAF No. 40561	RAF	Bf109	**W3579**	OU-Q	1.0	C
	Sgt Harvey N. **SWEETMAN**	NZ40992	RNZAF	Bf109	**AB860**	OU-U	1.0	C
17.09.41	F/L Edward P. **WELLS**	NZ39950	RNZAF	Bf109	**W3645**	OU-S	1.0	P
18.09.41	F/L Edward P. **WELLS**	NZ39950	RNZAF	Bf109	**W3645**	OU-S	1.0	C
	Sgt Harvey N. **SWEETMAN**	NZ40992	RNZAF	Bf109	**AB918**	OU-Y	1.0	C
	P/O Harold L. **THOMAS**	NZ391850	RNZAF	Bf109	**W3527**	OU-M	1.0	P
21.09.41	F/L Edward P. **WELLS**	NZ39950	RNZAF	Bf109	**W3645**	OU-S	2.0	C
	P/O Graham H. **FRANCIS**	NZ391834	RNZAF	Bf109	**AB870**	OU-Z	1.0	C
	P/O William V. **CRAWFORD-COMPTON**	RAF No. 65500	(NZ)/RAF	Bf109	**AB788**	OU-T	1.0	P
02.10.41	F/L Edward P. **WELLS**	NZ39950	RNZAF	Bf109	**W3652**	OU-K	1.0	P
	F/O Robert H. **STRANG**	RAF No. 79515	(NZ)/RAF	Bf109	**W3578**	OU-D	1.0	P
	Sgt John D. **RAE**	NZ402896	RNZAF	Bf109	**AD114**	OU-G	1.0	P
13.10.41	P/O William V. **CRAWFORD-COMPTON**	RAF No. 65500	(NZ)/RAF	Bf109	**P8786**		1.0	C
21.10.41	Sgt Andrew S. **KRONFELD**	NZ402523	RNZAF	Bf109	**AB860**	OU-U	1.0	C
06.11.41	P/O William V. **CRAWFORD-COMPTON**	RAF No. 65500	(NZ)/RAF	Bf109	**W3774**	OU-R	1.0	P
	Sgt John D. **RAE**	NZ402896	RNZAF	Bf109	**AD114**	OU-G	1.0	P
12.02.42	F/L William V. **CRAWFORD-COMPTON**	RAF No. 65500	(NZ)/RAF	Bf109	**W3774**	OU-R	1.0	C
	P/O Reginald J.C. **GRANT**	NZ391352	RNZAF	Bf109	**W3528**	OU-C	1.0	C
	F/L Graham H. **FRANCIS**	NZ391834	RNZAF	Fw190	**BL385**	OU-F	1.0	C
	P/O Harvey N. **SWEETMAN**	NZ40992	RNZAF	Bf109	**AB860**	OU-U	0.5	C
	P/O David T. **CLOUSTON**	NZ404337	RNZAF		**W3577**	OU-P	0.5	C
	Sgt John D. **RAE**	NZ402896	RNZAF	Bf109	**AD114**	OU-G	1.0	P
03.03.42	W/C Donald O. **FINLAY**	RAF No. 36031	RAF	Bf109	**AB860**	OU-U	1.0	C
09.03.42	P/O Martin R.D. **HUME**	NZ405335	RNZAF	Fw190	**AD248**	OU-A	1.0	P
26.03.42	F/L William V. **CRAWFORD-COMPTON**	RAF No. 65500	(NZ)/RAF	Bf109	**W3774**	OU-R	1.0	C
				Bf109	**W3774**	OU-R	0.5	C
	P/O Evan D. **MACKIE**	NZ41520	RNZAF		**AB790**	OU-Q	0.5	C
	Sgt Irvine P.J. **MASKILL**	NZ41487	RNZAF	Bf109	**W3640**	OU-S	1.0	C
28.03.42	F/L William V. **CRAWFORD-COMPTON**	RAF No. 65500	(NZ)/RAF	Fw190	**W3774**	OU-R	1.0	C
	F/L Reginald J.C. **GRANT**	NZ391352	RNZAF	Fw190	**W3528**	OU-C	1.0	C
				Fw190	**W3528**	OU-C	1.0	P
	Sgt John D. **RAE**	NZ402896	RNZAF	Fw190	**AD114**	OU-G	1.0	C
	P/O John J. **PALMER**	NZ404402	RNZAF	Fw190	**W3407**	OU-Y	1.0	P
04.04.42	P/O Ian J. **McNEIL**	NZ401774	RNZAF	Fw190	**BM196**	OU-B	1.0	P
24.04.42	S/L Edward P. **WELLS**	NZ39950	RNZAF	Fw190	**BM229**	OU-A	1.0	C
	F/L William V. **CRAWFORD-COMPTON**	RAF No. 65500	(NZ)/RAF	Fw190	**BM234**	OU-R	1.0	C
	P/O John J. **PALMER**	NZ404402	RNZAF	Fw190	**BM151**	OU-Y	1.0	P

Top right, Pilot Officer 'Reg' Baker posing in front of Spitfire BL385/OU-F, an aircraft usually flown however by the A Flight Leader, F/L G.H. Francis in the beginning of 1942.
(via P. Sortehaug)

In the middle, Flight Sergeant A.R. Robson in Spitfire BM155/OU-U in April 1942. He would become a PoW on 13 February 1943.
(via P. Sortehaug)

Below Spitfire V BM464/OU-G usually flown by Pilot Officer E.D. Mackie in the spring of 1942.
(via P. Sortehaug)

Above, Spitfire BM208/OU-S being manoeuvred at Kingscliffe at the end of 1942. The pilot seated in the aircraft is Sgt C.J. Sheddan, later OC 486 (NZ) Sqn at the end of the war.

26.04.42	P/O Evan D. **MACKIE**	NZ41520	RNZAF	Fw190	**BM205**	OU-H	1.0	P
27.04.42	F/Sgt Anthony R. **ROBSON**	NZ403990	RNZAF	Fw190	**BM155**	OU-U	1.0	P
04.05.42	F/Sgt Anthony R. **ROBSON**	NZ403990	RNZAF	Fw190	**BM155**	OU-U	1.0	C
	F/L Michael M. **SHAND**	NZ391368	RNZAF	Fw190	**BM208**	OU-S	1.0	P
03.08.42	F/O Lindsay S. **BLACK**	NZ40961	RNZAF	Do217	**BM208**	OU-S	1.0	C
19.08.42	W/C Patrick G. **JAMESON**	RAF No. 37813	(NZ)/RAF	Fw190	**BM232**		1.0	C
	P/O Collin **CHRYSTALL**	RAF No. 46538	(NZ)/RAF	Fw190	**BM205**	OU-H	1.0	C
28.11.42	S/L Reginald J.C. **GRANT**	NZ391352	RNZAF	He115	**BM147**	OU-F	1.0	C
26.01.43	W/C Peter M. **BROTHERS**	RAF No. 37668	RAF	Fw190	**BL907**		1.0	C
13.02.43	S/L Reginald J.C. **GRANT**	NZ391352	RNZAF	Fw190	**BM147**	OU-F	1.0	C
	F/O Martin R.D. **HUME**	NZ405335	RNZAF	Fw190	**EP277**	OU-H	1.0	C
21.04.43	Sgt Gordon H. **MEAGHER**	NZ416139	RNZAF	Bf109	**BM205**		1.0	C

SPITFIRE MK IX

14.07.43	W/C Alan C. **DEERE**	RAF No. 40370	(NZ)/RAF	Fw190	**EN568**	AL	1.0	P
15.07.43	F/O John D. **RAE**	NZ402896	RNZAF	Fw190	**EN576**	OU-S	1.0	C
				Fw190			1.0	P
	S/L John M. **CHECKETTS**	NZ403602	RNZAF	Fw190	**EN572**	OU-H	1.0	C
	P/O Hugh S. **TUCKER**	NZ415042	RNZAF	Fw190	**EN529**	OU-Y	1.0	P
27.07.43	S/L John M. **CHECKETTS**	NZ403602	RNZAF	Fw190	**EN572**	OU-H	2.0	C
	F/Sgt Walter T.H. **STRAHAN**	NZ411468	RNZAF	Fw190	**BS543**	OU-F	1.0	C
	F/O John D. **RAE**	NZ402896	RNZAF	Fw190	**EN576**	OU-S	0.5	C
	P/O Hugh S. **TUCKER**	NZ415042	RNZAF		**JK860**	OU-P	0.5	C

31.07.43	S/L John M. **Checketts**	NZ403602	RNZAF	Bf109	**EN572**	OU-H	1.0	C
09.08.43	S/L John M. **Checketts**	NZ403602	RNZAF	Bf109	**EN572**	OU-H	3.0	C
				Bf109			1.0	P
	F/O John D. **Rae**	NZ402896	RNZAF	Bf109	**JK762**	OU-W	1.0	C
	F/O Bruce E. **Gibbs**	NZ402468	RNZAF	Bf109	**EN563**	OU-C	1.0	C
	P/O Hugh S. **Tucker**	NZ415042	RNZAF	Bf109	**EN634**	OU-B	1.0	C
17.08.43	F/O John D. **Rae**	NZ402896	RNZAF	Bf109	**EN560**	OU-T	2.0	C
19.08.43	F/L Martin R.D. **Hume**	NZ405335	RNZAF	Bf109	**EN554**	OU-K	1.0	C
22.08.43	F/O John D. **Rae**	NZ402896	RNZAF	Fw190	**JL223**	OU-Y	1.0	C
	F/Sgt Leslie S.McQ. **White**	NZ413919	RNZAF	Fw190	**BS543**	OU-S	1.0	C
27.08.43	P/O John A. **Houlton**	NZ413543	RNZAF	Fw190	**MH350**	OU-V	1.0	C
06.09.43	S/L John M. **Checketts**	NZ403602	RNZAF	Fw190	**EN572**	OU-H	1.0	C
				Fw190			1.0	P
16.09.43	F/L Bruce E. **Gibbs**	NZ402468	RNZAF	Fw190	**EN560**	OU-T	1.0	C
	F/O Murray **Metcalfe**	NZ413876	RNZAF	Fw190	**EN529**	OU-Y	1.0	C
	P/O John A. **Houlton**	NZ413543	RNZAF	Bf109	**MH350**	OU-V	0.5	C
	W/O Bert S. **Wapiti**	NZ41388	RNZAF		**JK769**	OU-M	0.5	C
03.10.43	W/O Bert S. **Wapiti**	NZ41388	RNZAF	Fw190	**JK769**	OU-M	0.5	C
	F/Sgt George C. **Couper**	NZ417026	RNZAF		**MH350**	OU-V	0.5	C
	F/O James E. **Mortimer**	NZ412259	(NZ)/RAF	Fw190	**MH490**	OU-P	1.0	C
06.06.44	F/O John A. **Houlton**	NZ413543	RNZAF	Ju88	**MK950**	OU-X	1.0	C
	F/O John A. **Houlton**	NZ413543	RNZAF	Ju88	**MK950**	OU-X	0.25	C
	F/L Keith J. **Macdonald**	NZ40981	RNZAF		**MK732**	OU-U	0.25	C
	F/O Maurice C. **Mayston**	NZ422304	RNZAF		**MK897**	OU-R	0.25	C
	F/Sgt Edward G. **Atkins**	NZ422246	RNZAF		**ML377**	OU-Y	0.25	C
08.06.44	F/O John A. **Houlton**	NZ413543	RNZAF	Bf109	**ML407**	OU-V	1.0	C
	F/O Allan B. **Stead**	NZ411996	RNZAF	Fw190	**ML950**	OU-X	1.0	C
	P/O Herbert W.B. **Patterson**	NZ415713	RNZAF	Bf109	**MK732**	OU-U	1.0	C
	F/O John F.P. **Yeatman**	NZ411965	RNZAF	Fw190	**MK677**	OU-A	0.5	C
	F/Sgt Maurice H. **Eyre**	NZ421692	RNZAF		**ML368**	OU-C	0.5	C
	P/O Frank **Transom**	NZ416575	RNZAF	Bf109	**ML754**	OU-N	1.0	C
12.06.44	F/L William A. **Newenham**	NZ39869	RNZAF	Bf109	**ML377**	OU-Y	1.0	C
	F/O John A. **Houlton**	NZ413543	RNZAF	Bf109	**ML407**	OU-V	1.0	C

Total: 95.0

Another future ace who served with 485 Sqn early on was P/O E.D. 'Rosie' Mackie. He completed his first tour with 485, but did not score much.
(A. Thomas)

William Marcus Bower KNIGHT
RAF No. 37408

Marcus Knight left New Zealand in 1935 to join the RAF. After his training he became a flying instructor and was still an instructor, a Flight commander of No. 5 Service Flight Training School with more than 1,000 hours of flying experience, when the war broke out. After the Battle of Britain the RAF was short of fighter pilots so, to help replace those who had been killed, injured or posted away for rest, he was sent, in December 1940, to undertake fighter training at No. 57 OTU. In January 1941 he was posted to No. 257 (Burma) Squadron as a flight commander. The next month he was transferred to No. 310 (Czech) Squadron, again as a Flight commander, and in March he was given the task of forming the first New Zealand fighter unit in the RAF, No. 485 (NZ) Squadron. He was a good candidate and in a month, had the squadron operational. Then on 2 June, 1941, he shot down the first German aircraft claimed by the New Zealanders. In October he added a damaged claim to his credit and was awarded the DFC. At the end of November 1941 he relinquished command of the squadron. No more operational postings followed and he served in various administrative positions in the UK and Middle East. He was a Group Captain at the cessation of hostilities. He remained in the RAF after the war.

Supermarine Spitfire Mk V AB870
No. 485 (NZ) Squadron
Squadron Leader WMB Knight
Redhill (UK), summer 1941

Edward Preston WELLS
NZ39950

'Hawkeye' Wells joined the RNZAF in October 1939. Upon completion of training, he was posted to No. 266 Squadron in August 1940, then to No. 41 Squadron in October. With No.41 Squadron he shot down three Bf109s and was also involved in repelling the Italian raid targeting British shipping on 11th November 1940, during which he engaged and damaged a Fiat CR42. He became a founder member of No. 485 (NZ) Squadron in March 1941 and rapidly rose through the ranks, becoming a flight commander and, in November, it's Commanding Officer. During his service with the New Zealand Spitfire Squadron he was credited with eight confirmed victories, twice achieving a double on a single operation, once on the 5th July and again on 21st September 1941. For his successes with Nos. 41 and 485 Squadrons he received the DFC in August 1941, and a Bar in November. During May 1942 he was appointed Wing Leader of the Kenley Wing, being rested three months later. He was awarded the DSO in August, becoming the first New Zealander to hold the DSO, DFC & Bar. He returned to operations in 1943 and became the Wing Leader again of Kenley, between August and November, after which he was posted to HQ 11 Group. In March 1944 he flew as supernumerary Wing Commander with No. 144 Wing, adding a last claim on 28 March. This brought his total to twelve enemy aircraft confirmed, four probable, and seven damaged, one of which was shared. In mid-May he became WingCo flying of Detling Wing, the West Malling Wing in July, and finally the Hawkinge Wing in August. At the beginning of November he became tour expired. Wells was released from the RNZAF in 1947 to take a permanent commission in the RAF, retiring as a Group Captain in 1960.

Supermarine Spitfire Mk V W3645
No. 485 (NZ) Squadron
Flight Lieutenant EP Wells
Redhill (UK), autumn 1941

'Bill' Crawford-Compton left his native New Zealand in 1939 to join the RAF. He arrived in England shortly after the declaration of war and enlisted in the RAF in October. By the end of 1940, he had been posted to 57 OTU and, on completion of that course, was posted to No. 603 (City of Edinburgh) Squadron as an NCO in the early days of January 1941. Soon after, he became a founding member of No. 485 (NZ) Squadron, formed in March 1941, and received his commission in May. He had to wait until 21 September to open his score by claiming a Bf109 probably destroyed. During the next 12 months, he became the second most successful of 485's pilots, assuming a flight commander's position in January 1942 and being awarded the DFC in March, but the following month was involved in an accident which saw him removed from operations for a short while.

Recovered by August, he was posted to No. 611 (West Lancashire) Squadron as a flight commander and was again very successful until he was given command of No. 64 Squadron in December, a position he assumed with a Bar to his DFC awarded the previous month. In March 1943, he was rested until June when he became wing leader of the Hornchurch Wing. In October, he left the wing with a DSO and, six months later, was given another command, wing leader of No. 145 Wing of 2TAF. It is at the head of this wing that Crawford-Compton made his last claim – a Bf109 destroyed over Normandy – to bring his tally to 20 confirmed victories, (one shared), six probables and 12 damaged. He eventually left the wing in January 1945 with a Bar to his DSO. Bill Crawford-Compton emerged as one of New Zealand's most highly decorated fighter pilots of the war. Continuing his career, he eventually reached the rank of Air Vice-Marshal before retiring in November 1968.

Supermarine Spitfire Mk V W3774
No. 485 (NZ) Squadron
Flight Lieutenant WV Crawford-Compton
Redhill (UK), autumn 1941

Enlisting in the RAF on a short service commission, Norris was serving with No. 66 Squadron at the outbreak of war. He was then posted to No. 610 (County of Chester) Squadron during September. He made his first claim over Dunkirk, a Bf109 destroyed, on the 29th and later took part in the Battle of Britain, being awarded the DFC in September 1940 while rising to become a flight commander. He had also steadily increased his tally during that period. In April 1941, he was rested but returned to operations in August as a flight commander with No. 485 (NZ) Squadron upon its formation. He was then sent overseas and took command of No. 126 Squadron on Malta in December. He left 126 in April 1942 for another rest, having made his final claim a bit before when he damaged a Ju88. His score had reached nine confirmed victories (one shared), two probables and four damaged. Resuming operations in 1942, Norris assumed command of No. 33 Squadron in the Western Desert in November, remaining in the role until February 1943. He was eventually posted to India in August and the following month took command of No. 11 Squadron, staying until March 1944, and adding a Bar to his DFC in May. He served in the Far East until the end of the war with the rank of wing commander.

Supermarine Spitfire Mk V W3579
No. 485 (NZ) Squadron
Flight Lieutenant SC Norris
Redhill (UK), summer 1941

Wing Commander Norman Ryder, Wing Leader of Kenley Wing, was flying with F/L Norris's Spitfire V W3579/OU-Q in the surf near Dunkirk after being hit by flak. Ryder was leading 485 Squadron on this occasion and became a prisoner. He had the DFC & Bar and had claimed eight victories, one of which was shared, all while serving with 41 Squadron.
(Andrew Thomas)

Reginald William BAKER
NZ401748

'Reg' Baker enlisted in the RNZAF in July 1940. Trained in New Zealand, he sailed to the UK with a commission in February 1941. In May, he attended 53 OTU shortly after arrival, at the end of which he was posted to No. 485 (NZ) Squadron in July, recently formed. In May 1942, he became a flight commander and was awarded the DFC in September. He held this position until he took over the squadron in March 1943. In July, he was rested and posted to No 11 Group HQ as a staff officer. After a twin-engine conversion course, he started a second tour of operations in January 1945 as OC of No. 487 (NZ) Squadron, flying Mosquito Mk VIs. He was killed in action soon after, on 22 February 1945 during a day intruder mission near Humburg in Germany.

Supermarine Spitfire Mk V BM233
No. 485 (NZ) Squadron
Kingscliffe (UK), summer-autumn 1942

Date	Pilot	S/N	Origin	Serial	Code	Fate
			SPITFIRE MK I			
09.05.41	Sgt James K. **PORTEOUS**	NZ401030	RNZAF	**X4903**	OU-Z	-
			SPITFIRE MK II			
23.06.41	Sgt Richard J. **BULLEN**	NZ40753	RNZAF	**P7975**	OU-R	†
08.07.41	Sgt William N. **HENDRY**	NZ39067	RNZAF	**P8470**	OU-S	†
11.07.41	P/O Charles **STEWART**	RAF No. 44231	(NZ)/RAF	**P7773**	OU-D	†
24.07.41	Sgt Jack **MANEY**	NZ40240	RNZAF	**P7831**	OU-G	†
07.08.41	Sgt Charles S.V. **GOODWIN**	NZ401758	RNZAF	**P7594**	OU-G	**PoW**
12.08.41	Sgt George M. **PORTER**	RAF No. 931283	(NZ)/RAF	**P7788**	OU-E	†
	Sgt William H. **RUSSELL***	NZ40987	RNZAF	**P7970**	OU-D	**PoW**
19.08.41	Sgt Keith C.M. **MILLER**	NZ401761	RNZAF	**P7977**	OU-U	†

** Severely wounded and repatriated in October 1943*

Date	Pilot	S/N	Origin	Serial	Code	Fate
			SPITFIRE MK V			
27.08.41	F/O William A. **MIDDLETON**	NZ39928	RNZAF	**W3527**	OU-M	†
29.08.41	Sgt Lyndon P. **GRIFFITHS**	NZ40968	RNZAF	**W3643**	OU-C	-
18.09.41	F/Sgt Arthur I. **PAGET**	NZ402211	RNZAF	**AB903**		†
21.09.41	P/O John F. **KNIGHT**	NZ403456	RNZAF	**AB856**	OU-E	**PoW**
31.10.41	W/C Edgar N. **RYDER**	RAF No. 39193	RAF	**W3579**	OU-Q	**PoW**
29.12.41	P/O John J. **PALMER**	NZ404402	RNZAF	**AB853**	OU-F	-
25.01.42	F/L Robert H. **STRANG**	RAF No. 79515	(NZ)/RAF	**AB788**	OU-T	†
26.03.42	F/Sgt William M. **KREBS**	NZ402194	RNZAF	**W3577**	OU-P	†
04.04.42	P/O Edward F. **CHANDLER**	NZ402543	RNZAF	**BM231**	OU-C	†
	P/O Thomas T. **FOX**	NZ411392	RNZAF	**P8724**	OU-A	†
26.04.42	F/Sgt John R. **LIKEN**	NZ404385	RNZAF	**BM139**	OU-E	†
	F/Sgt Travis C. **GOODLET**	NZ403546	RNZAF	**BM290**	OU-G	**PoW**
	F/O John G. **PATTISON**	NZ39931	RNZAF	**BM267**	OU-N	-
	P/O Lloyd M. **RALPH**	NZ401779	RNZAF	**BM197**	OU-P	-
27.04.42	P/O John J. **PALMER**	NZ404402	RNZAF	**BM151**	OU-Y	**PoW**
	F/L William V. **CRAWFORD-COMPTON**	RAF No. 65500	(NZ)/RAF	**BM234**	OU-R	-
01.05.42	P/O John R. **FALLS**	NZ41509	RNZAF	**BM116**	OU-Y	**PoW**
04.05.42	W/O David M. **RUSSELL**	NZ403553	RNZAF	**BM196**	OU-B	†
	P/O John M. **CHECKETTS**	NZ403602	RNZAF	**BM259**	OU-D	-
31.05.42	F/L Matthew G. **BARNETT**	NZ391338	RNZAF	**BL383**	OU-A	Eva.
	Sgt Stanley F. **BROWNE**	NZ411853	RNZAF	**BL699**	OU-L	Eva.
22.07.42	P/O Harold W. **HARRISON**	RAF No. 48001	RAF	**BL815**	OU-M	†
02.08.42	Sgt Norman N. **LANGLANDS**	NZ412702	RNZAF	**BM247**	OU-T	†
03.08.42	Sgt Ronald W. **VESSEY**	NZ413156	RNZAF	**BM183**	OU-D	†
01.09.42	Sgt Richard D. **RILEY**	NZ413479	RNZAF	**BM239**	OU-N	**PoW**
28.11.42	Sgt Francis W. **NORRIS**	NZ412724	RNZAF	**BM232**	OU-Y	†
	F/L Michael M. **SHAND**	NZ391368	RNZAF	**EP595**	Squn-Q	**PoW**
06.02.43	P/O Laurence B. **GORDON**	NZ414281	RNZAF	**BM513**	OU-K	**PoW**
13.02.43	F/O Ian A.C. **GRANT**	NZ391351	RNZAF	**BM482**	OU-W	†

	Sgt Revell J. **Steed**	NZ414354	RNZAF	**EP115**	OU-R	†
	F/O Anthony R. **Robson**	NZ403990	RNZAF	**EP107**	OU-U	**PoW**
04.04.43	Sgt Hubert J. **Oxley**	NZ412725	RNZAF	**BM208**	OU-S	†
13.04.43	Sgt Thomas W.J. **Denholm**	NZ415687	RNZAF	**BM299**		†
30.05.43	F/O George J. **Moorhead**	NZ412256	RNZAF	**BM378**	OU-B	†

Spitfire Mk IX

14.07.43	Capt John R. **Walker**	O-439347	USAAF	**EN564**	OU-T	†
15.07.43	F/Sgt Terence S.F. **Kearins**	NZ404877	RNZAF	**EN573**	OU-Y	†
22.08.43	F/O Malcolm G. **Sutherland**	NZ413506	RNZAF	**EN634**	OU-B	**PoW**
	F/O John D. **Rae**	NZ402896	RNZAF	**JL223**	OU-Y	**PoW**
	P/O Fraser D. **Clarke**	NZ414590	RNZAF	**EN631**	OU-E	†
	F/Sgt Leslie S.McQ. **White**	NZ413919	RNZAF	**BS543**	OU-F	**Eva.**
06.09.43	S/L John M. **Checketts**	NZ403602	RNZAF	**EN572**	OU-H	**Eva.**
16.09.43	F/O Murray **Metcalfe**	NZ413876	RNZAF	**EN529**	OU-Y	†
24.09.43	F/O John A. **Ainge**	NZ415279	RNZAF	**MH470**		†
03.10.43	W/O Bert S. **Wapiti**	NZ41388	RNZAF	**JK769**	OU-M	†
	F/O James E. **Mortimer**	NZ412259	RNZAF	**MH490**	OU-P	**Eva.**
	F/Sgt Neville E. **Frehner**	NZ415409	RNZAF	**MH351**		†
20.10.43	F/O John G. **Thomson**	NZ413510	RNZAF	**EN559**	OU-U	†
	F/O Ronald L. **Baker**	NZ391337	RNZAF	**JK762**	OU-W	†
	F/Sgt Frank **Transom**	NZ416575	RNZAF	**MH364**	OU-S	-
01.01.45	*Destroyed on the ground*	-	-	**MK722**	OU-W	-
	Destroyed on the ground	-	-	**MK921**		-
	Destroyed on the ground	-	-	**ML361**		-
	Destroyed on the ground	-	-	**NH321**		-
	Destroyed on the ground	-	-	**NH421**		-
	Destroyed on the ground	-	-	**NH432**	OU-D	-
	Destroyed on the ground	-	-	**NH530**	OU-F	-
	Destroyed on the ground	-	-	**PL251**	OU-L	-
	Destroyed on the ground	-	-	**PT857**		-
	Destroyed on the ground	-	-	**PT890**	OU-G	-
	Destroyed on the ground	-	-	**PV156**	OU-H	-
06.01.45	F/L Allan B. **Stead**	NZ411996	RNZAF	**PL394**	OU-H	†
	F/O Francis C. **Matthews**	NZ4211615	RNZAF	**NH514**	OU-U	†
08.02.45	F/O Donald G.L. **Taylor**	NZ427048	RNZAF	**MK529**	OU-D	†
13.02.45	F/O Maxwell A. **Collett**	NZ422260	RNZAF	**PT856**	OU-A	-

Total: 73

The wreckage of the Spitfire flown by F/Sgt L.S.M. White (BS543/OU-F) who was shot down on 22 August 1943. He evaded capture and returned to the UK.

Three Spitfires which were destroyed on 1 January 1945, NH530/OU-F, NH432:OU-D and PV156/OU-H. The remains of the latter are contemplated by his regular pilot, F/O Don Taylor. *(via P. Sortehaug)*

Flight Lieutenant M.G. Barnett discussing aerial tactics with P/O M. Metcalfe (left) and F/L L.S. Black (right) in early 1943. 'Killer' Metcalfe did not survive the war and was killed in action on 16 September 1943. *(via P. Sortehaug)*

Sgt 'Dick' Bullen jumping into his Spitfire. He was the first 485's operational casualty of the war in being posted missing after an escort mission to St-Omer on 23 June 1941, and left, the last one, 'Don' Taylor on 8 February 1945.
(via P. Sortehaug)

Squadron Leader 'Reg' Grant, the CO, with his two flight commanders. Left, 'Reg' Baker succeeded Grant at the head of A Flight. He was lost at the head of 487 (NZ) Squadron while flying a Mosquito on 22 February 1945. On his right is 'Mick' Shand, the B Flight CO. He became a PoW in November 1944 and would take part in the Great Escape in March 1944. Recaptured, he was not executed. Grant was killed flying a Mustang as wing leader of 122 Wing on 28 February 1944. *(via P. Sortehaug)*

Reginald Joseph Cowan GRANT
NZ391352

'Reg' Grant joined the RNZAF in November 1939. He was shipped to the UK to complete his training, joining No. 145 Squadron in April 1941 as an NCO after attending 53 OTU. He opened his score soon after on 21 June by claiming a Bf109 destroyed over the Channel. Two more claims were made before he was posted to No. 485 (NZ) Squadron in October 1941 with a DFM. At the end of the year, he received his commission, followed by a promotion when he became a flight commander in February 1942; in May, he took command of the squadron. In the following weeks, he made further claims and was awarded the DFC in September. He led 485 until March 1943 when he was rested, receiving a Bar to his DFC shortly thereafter in June. In November 1943, Grant started another tour and was given command of No. 65 Squadron, only to be promoted again and assume the role of wing leader of 122 Airfield (of which 65 Squadron was a part) in January 1944. On 21 January, he made his final claim, a shared Me210 destroyed over France, to bring his total to eight confirmed victories (one shared) and one probable. Shortly after, he converted to the Mustang. Sadly, on 28 February, while taking off to lead the wing on an escort mission, the engine of his Mustang suffered trouble and he was seen to crash a few miles east of Gravesend, losing his life in the process.

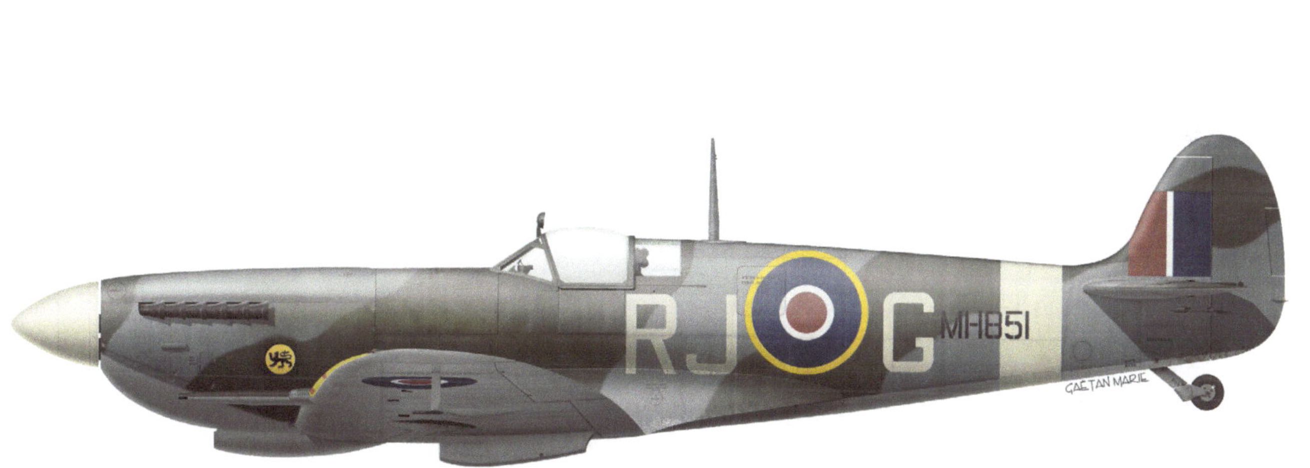

Supermarine Spitfire Mk IX MH851
No. 122 Airfield
Wing Commander RJC Grant
Gravesend (UK), January-February 1944

John Milne CHECKETTS
NZ403602

'Johnny' Checketts enlisted in the RNZAF in October 1940, completing his initial training in New Zealand. In July 1941 he sailed for the UK, attending 56 OTU shortly after arrival. During November he was posted to No. 485 (NZ) Squadron, but found the going tough and was shot down on 4 May 1942 by Fw190s, bailing out over the Channel. He was picked up however within an hour. The following month he completed a course at the Central Gunnery School and afterwards became a gunnery instructor. In January 1943 he joined No. 611 (West Lancashire) Squadron and immediately began scoring. He damaged a Fw190 on 13 January, and at the end of June, by which time he had been made a flight commander, he had three Focke-Wulfs confirmed and four damaged. In July he was promoted to Squadron Leader to take command of 485 and the following month he was awarded the DFC. In a short time he achieved considerable success with the Kiwis and by the end of August had raised his total to 10 confirmed victories, including three on one sortie. On 6 September, he was himself shot down over France, baling out with various wounds and burns. Hidden by French civilians he was able to avoid capture, and the French Resistance arranged his repatriation to England, which he reached seven weeks after his downing. He was made companion of the DSO, and in April 1944 was given command of No. 1 Squadron. At the end of the following month, he became Wing Leader of No. 142 Wing, with which he would make his last claims, to bring his score to 13 aircraft destroyed, (one shared), two probably destroyed, and ten damaged and additionally he destroyed two V-1s. He remained with the wing until the end of September, it being his last operational posting. He was repatriated at the end of 1945, continuing service with the RNZAF until March 1954.

Supermarine Spitfire Mk VC AB509
No. 142 Wing
Wing Commander JM Checketts
Friston (UK), May-June 1944

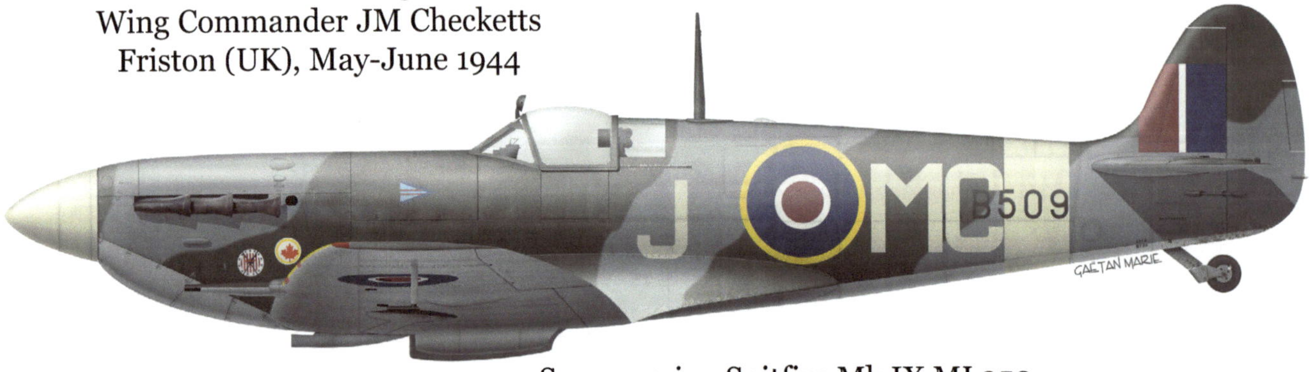

Supermarine Spitfire Mk IX ML350
No. 142 Wing
Wing Commander JM Checketts
B.61/St.Denis-Westrem (Belgium), September 1944

Johnny Checketts' Spitfire V AB509, he used when he was Wing Leader of No. 142 Wing in the spring of 1944. Below his Spitfire Mk IX, ML350 he later flew.
(Paul Sortehaug)

John Donald RAE
NZ402896

'Jack' Rae enlisted in the RNZAF in September 1940. Upon completing his training, he was sent to England to attend 61 OTU in April 1941, at the end of which he was posted to No. 485 (NZ) Squadron as an NCO. He opened his score on 12 August when he claimed a Bf109 damaged over the French coast. Six more claims followed before he decided to serve overseas and, consequently, in April 1942, was posted to No. 603 (City of Edinburgh) Squadron, which was about to leave for Malta, reaching the island at the end of the month. Shot down and wounded during his first engagements, he returned to operations in June, but with No. 249 (Gold Coast) Squadron. During the summer, he steadily increased his tally and was also commissioned. In August, Rae was posted back to the UK for a rest. In December, he was awarded the DFC.

His second tour of operations began in May 1943 with a return to 485 Squadron. He rapidly claimed further victories, the last on 22 August when he destroyed an Fw190 near Le Havre, bringing his scoreboard to 13 confirmed victories (two shared), nine probably destroyed (one shared) and six damaged. After he had shot down this last Fw190, however, he experienced an engine failure and was forced to come down in France. He spent the rest of the war as a PoW with a Bar added to his DFC in September 1943.

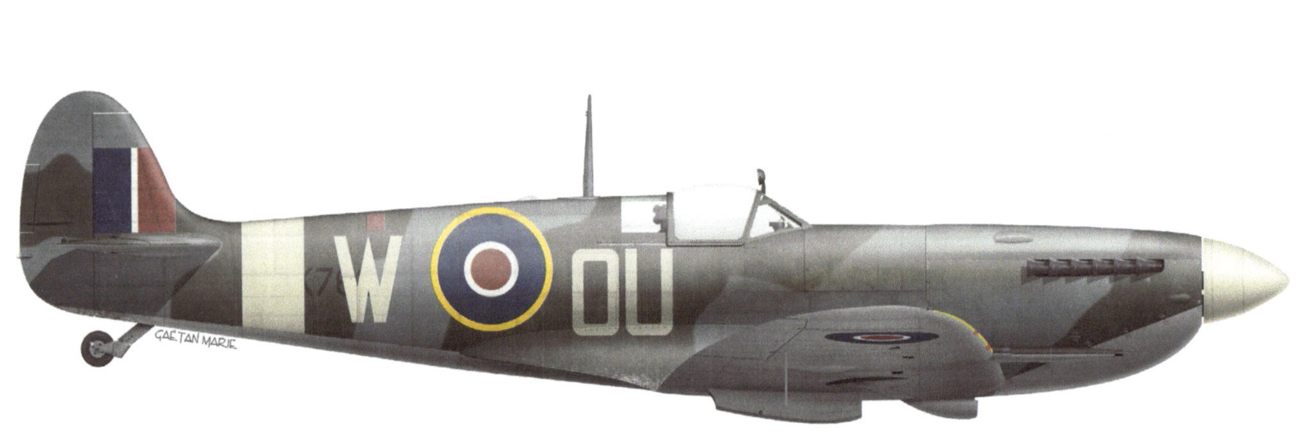

Supermarine Spitfire Mk IXB JK762
No. 485 (NZ) Squadron
Biggin Hill (UK), summer 1943

Martin Robert Draycott HUME
NZ405335

'Marty' Hume was a New Zealander of Māori parentage. He volunteered for the RNZAF in December 1940 and, on completion of his training, was posted to the UK during the autumn of 1941. He attended 58 OTU and on graduation was posted to No. 485 (NZ) Squadron in December. He progressively held various key positions within the squadron, such as flight leader between March and September 1943, and finally served as CO between September 1943 and February 1944. In the meantime, he had opened his score on 9 March 1942 with a Fw190 probably destroyed. Tour-expired in February 1944, he was posted out for a rest. In January 1945, he was given another command, No. 130 (Punjab) Squadron, to start a second tour of operations. He led 130 until April 1945, just after he had made his last claim of the war, a Ju188 destroyed on the 10th. He returned to the UK that evening with a tally of three confirmed victories, one probable and one damaged. In May, he was awarded the DFC. Hume left the RNZAF in December 1945.

Supermarine Spitfire Mk IX MH819
No. 485 (NZ) Squadron
Hornchurch (UK), October 1943

John Arthur HOULTON
NZ413543

Joining the RNZAF in June 1941, Houlton completed his training and sailed for the UK in the spring of 1942 where he attended 55 OTU. As an NCO, he joined No. 485 (NZ) Squadron as his first operational assignment in June 1942. His stay was brief, however, as he volunteered for service in Malta and arrived on the island in August 1942, joining No. 185 Squadron, but soon suffered severe sinus trouble followed by a bout of ill health in September and October. It was not until November, therefore, that he could fly regularly. On the 28th, he damaged two Ju52s over the Mediterranean, his first claims. The following month, he opted to return to England where he joined No. 602 (City of Glasgow) Squadron in January 1943 before being transferred back to 485 in February. In July, he was finally commissioned and soon after achieved his first confirmed kill. On 6 June 1944, Houlton was one the few pilots to score over the D-Day beaches by claiming one Ju88 destroyed and sharing in the destruction of another. He continued to increase his tally during the summer until he became tour-expired in September, leaving with a DFC. In April 1945, he returned to operations as a flight commander with No. 274 Squadron, flying the Tempest, with which he made his last claim – a Do217 shot down near Kiel. His final score was seven confirmed victories (two shared) and four damaged.

Supermarine Spitfire Mk IX ML407
No. 485 (NZ) Squadron
Flight Lieutenant JA Houlton
Funtington (UK), July-August 1944

John Brown NIVEN
RAF NO. 109061

'Johnny' Niven enlisted in the RAF in June 1939. He attended No. 57 OTU and, upon completion of his training, was posted to No. 602 (City of Glasgow) Squadron in April 1941 as an NCO. He opened his score on 17 September when he claimed a Bf109 destroyed. He received a commission in November. By the end of December 1942, the end of his tour, he had increased his score to two confirmed victories, three probables and four aircraft damaged. This included two claims on 19 August over Dieppe (a probable Do217 and an Fw190 damaged). A DFC was awarded in May 1942.

Rested as a flight instructor, he started a new tour of operations in August 1943 as a flight commander with No. 322 (Dutch) Squadron before taking over No. 485 (NZ) Squadron in February 1944. He was to be the only non-New Zealander CO of this fighter squadron. He led the unit during the first stages of the invasion of the Continent and relinquished command in September. During this time, he made his last claim, an Fw190 damaged, on 8 June 1944. In December, he received a Bar to his DFC. He was sent to the Far East in June 1945 and served with No. 907 Wing until the end of the war but saw no action.

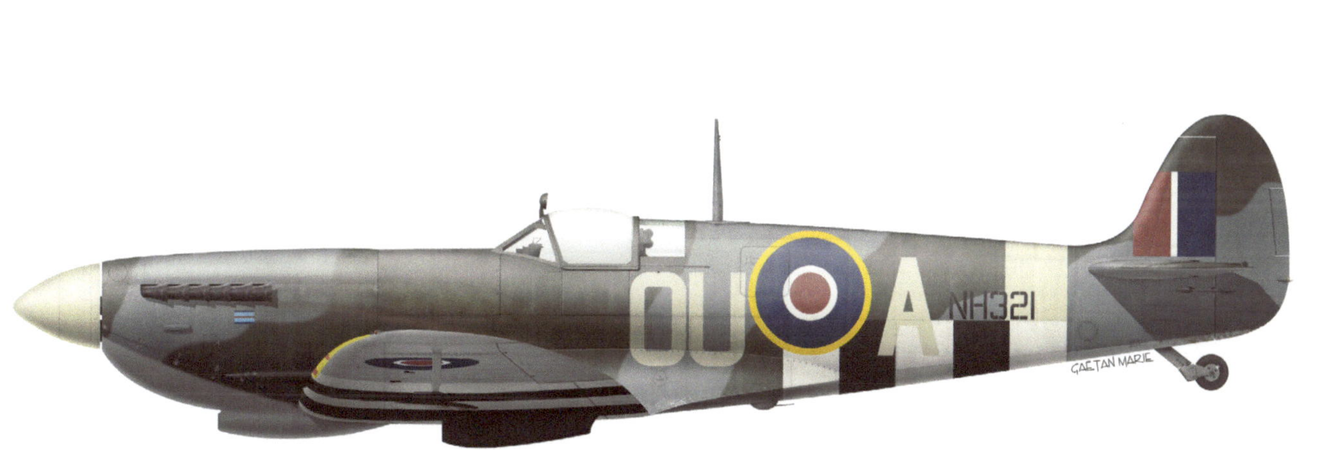

Supermarine Spitfire Mk IX NH321
No. 485 (NZ) Squadron
Squadron Leader JB Niven
B.17/Carpiquet (France), August 1944

A fuel malfunction caused the crash of PT532/OU-Q on 12 October 1944. The pilot, Pilot Officer TSF Kearins escaped injuries and the aircraft was repaired. Below, Spitfire Mk IX PT881/OU-T 'Thunderguts' in September-October 1944. It eventually left in December for unspecified causes. *(via P. Sortehaug)*

Above, Spitfire Mk IX MK288/OU-Q in December 1944.
Below, Spitfire Mk IX PT8857/OU-S, which was eventually destroyed in air raid on 1 January 1945.
(via P. Sortehaug)

John Gordon PATTISON
NZ39931

John Pattison enlisted in the RNZAF in October 1939. He was trained in New Zealand and sailed for the UK in June 1940. After converting onto Spitfires at 7 OTU, he joined No. 266 (Natal) Squadron at the end of August during the middle of the Battle of Britain. The following month he was posted to No. 92 (East India) Squadron but on 23 September was shot down by a Bf109 and severely wounded, spending the next eight months in hospitals. His only claim during the Battle was for one enemy aircraft damaged. In June 1941, after convalescence, he returned briefly to operations re-joining 92 Squadron. The following month, he was sent as a flying instructor. In March 1942, Pattison was posted to No. 485 (NZ) Squadron. In June he was appointed Air Liaison Officer at High Ercall, where American pilots were given training on Spitfires. He then returned to 485 Squadron in November, becoming a flight commander. He completed his tour, being rested in June 1943, and received a DFC. Again, he was appointed a flying instructor. During March 1944 he joined No. 66 Squadron, and was subsequently given charge of a flight. With this unit he was able to redress his two earlier claims by shooting down a Bf 109 on 6 July and a Fw190 on 12 August. In September, he was given command of 485 Squadron, holding the position until February 1945. No operational position followed and in May, he was made Companion of the DSO. Repatriated to New Zealand in January 1946, he left the RNZAF one year later.

Supermarine Spitfire Mk IX PT532
No. 485 (NZ) Squadron
B.53/Merville (France), October 1944

Above, Spitfire Mk IX NH604/OU-U in December 1944.
Below, Spitfire Mk IX MK804/OU-U in May 1945, a bit before the Mk XVI were taken on charge.
(via P. Sortehaug)

Date	Pilot	S/N	Origin	Serial	Code	Fate
		SPITFIRE MK I				
05.05.41	P/O William A. **MIDDLETON**	NZ39928	RNZAF	**X4609**	OU-C	-
		SPITFIRE MK II				
18.06.41	Sgt Kevin D. **COX**	NZ401257	RNZAF	**P7858**	OU-F	†
		SPITFIRE MK V				
26.09.41	Sgt William M. **KREBS**	NZ402194	RNZAF	**W3530**	OU-M	-
11.01.42	*Ground accident*	-	-	**W3578**	OU-D	-
15.04.42	Sgt Stanley F. **BROWNE**	NZ411853	RNZAF	**BL346**	OU-D	-
29.04.42	Sgt Hector R. **LECKIE**	NZ411909	RNZAF	**BM250**		-
15.07.42	P/O Bruce E. **GIBBS**	NZ402468	RNZAF	**BP858**		-
22.12.43	F/O John G. **DASENT**	NZ404342	RNZAF	**BL634**	OU-M	†
		SPITFIRE MK IX				
31.08.43	F/L Bruce E. **GIBBS**	NZ402468	RNZAF	**JK860**	OU-P	-
15.11.44	P/O Clinton **MCINNES**	NZ416511	RNZAF	**NH364**	OU-H	†
		SPITFIRE MK XVI				
19.06.45	P/O Maxwell A. **COLLETT**	NZ422260	RNZAF	**TB741**	OU-D	-

Total: 11

Flight Lieutenant B.E. Gibbs crashed while taking off from Biggin Hill on 31 August 1943. While he was unhurt, the Spitfire, JK960/P, was a total loss.
P/O Max Collett's Spitfire Mk.XVI OU-D TB741 in distraught state at Drope in Germany, after another aircraft collided with him while landing, 19 June 1945. Collett sustained slight injuries but resumed flying a week later. (*via P. Sortehaug*)

Keith James Macdonald
NZ40981

Having previously served with the RNZAF, as an engine apprentice between November 1936 and April 1937, Keith Macdonald volunteered for pilot training in April 1940. Following graduation in October he was commissioned and retained, as a flying instructor, in New Zealand for nearly two years. In 1942, when the RNZAF began expanding its operational arm, Macdonald was among those instructors released for combat service. In October, while attending an OTU, he collided with a Hawker Hind, he and the two Hind occupants, successfully parachuting to safety. This was said to be the first successful exit from a RNZAF P-40. At the beginning of December 1942 he joined No 16 Squadron, RNZAF, flying Kittyhawks, before transferring to No 18 Squadron, RNZAF in March 1943. Later that same month he was diverted to No 14 Squadron, RNZAF, which ferried its P-40s from New Zealand to the New Hebrides Islands. He completed a tour with 14 Squadron before being admitted to hospital having contracted malaria. Classified unfit for tropical service he was posted to the UK in September 1943 and in February 1944, after attending OTU, was directed to No 485 (NZ) Squadron, flying Spitfires, as a Flight Lieutenant. On 6 June, he shared in the destruction of a Ju88, his only confirmed claim of the war. In October, he was posted to No 222 (Natal) Squadron as a flight commander. He was awarded the DFC in February 1945 (gazetted May) and returned as Commanding Officer to 485 Squadron that same month. The New Zealanders were in the process of converting to Tempests, but a lack of these aircraft saw them revert back to Spitfire Mk. IXs, updating to the Mk. XVI soon after VE-Day. Macdonald remained at the head of the squadron until mid-July 1945, and was repatriated back home soon after. He was eventually released from the RNZAF in January 1946.

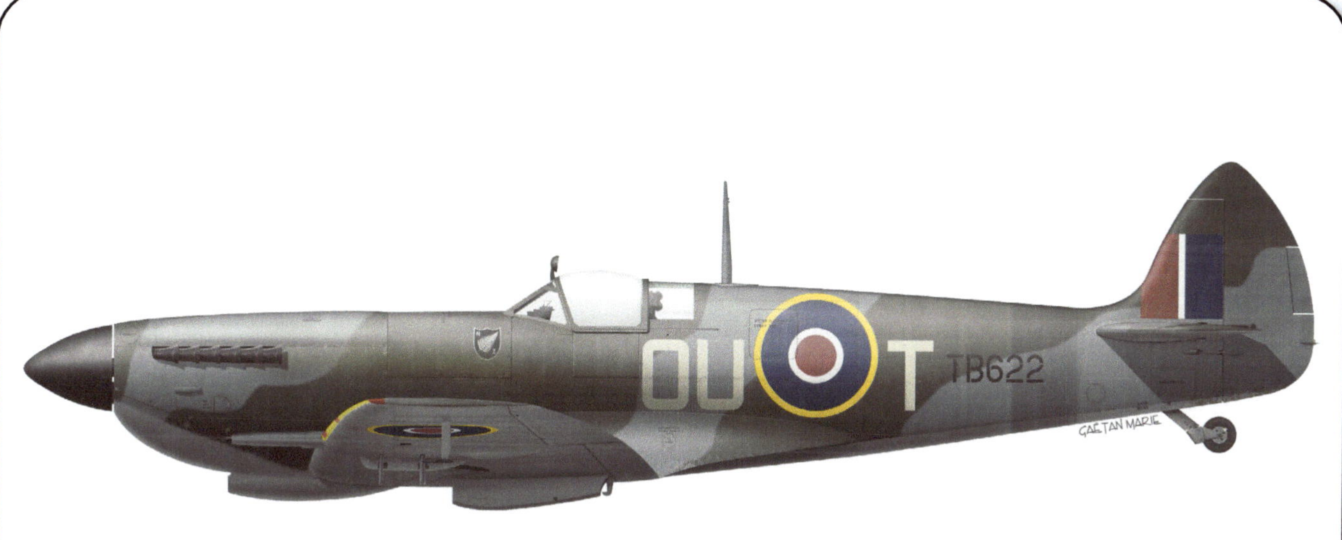

Supermarine Spitfire LF.XVI TB622
No. 485 (NZ) Squadron
Squadron Leader KJ Macdonald
B.105/Drope (Germany), June 1945

Stanley Franklin BROWNE
NZ411852

Stan Browne enlisted in the RNZAF in March 1941. Posted to England on completion of training, he joined 485 Squadron in March 1942 as an NCO. On 31 May, he was shot down over France, but he managed to evade capture and by November, he was back at the squadron. Browne was commissioned a pilot officer in January 1943 but on account of his spying activities while evading the Germans in France, it was deemed too risky for him to return to operations in Europe. He was then transferred to another theatre of operations, North Africa and eventually joined No. 93 Squadron in March. He opened his score soon afterwards, in claiming a Bf109 damaged over Tunisia. He increased his score the following months over Tunisia, Sicily and Southern Italy, making his last claim on 5 October, a Bf109 destroyed, bringing his tally to six confirmed victories, one being shared, and two aircraft damaged. The previous month, he had been awarded the DFC.

In December, his tour ended and returned to the UK. He started a second tour of operations in September 1944 with 485 again, as a flight commander. He held this position until being promoted to command in July 1945, leading the squadron until the disbandment of 485 in August. In September, he added a Bar to his DFC and eventually left the service in January 1946.

Supermarine Spitfire Mk XVI TB675
No. 485 (NZ) Squadron
B.105/Drope (Germany), summer 1945

Victories - confirmed or probable claims: 85.5 + 242.33 V-1s

First operational sortie:
27.04.42
Last operational sortie:
05.05.45

Number of sorties: *ca.* 10,800

Total aircraft written-off: 85

Aircraft lost on operations: 72
Aircraft lost in accidents: 13

Squadron code letters:
SA

COMMANDING OFFICERS

S/L Claude L.C. ROBERTS	RAF No. 37363	RAF	03.03.42	01.04.43
S/L Desmond J. SCOTT	NZ40779	RNZAF	01.04.43	25.09.43
S/L Ian D. WADDY	NZ402195	RNZAF	25.09.43	07.01.44
S/L James H. IREMONGER	RAF No. 33342	RAF	07.01.44	11.12.44
S/L Arthur E. UMBERS (†)	NZ404003	RNZAF	11.12.44	14.02.45
S/L Keith G. TAYLOR-CANNON (†)	NZ412284	RNZAF	15.02.45	13.04.45
S/L Warren E. SCHRADER	NZ411944	RNZAF	21.04.45	02.05.45
S/L Cornelius J. SHEDDAN	NZ412358	RNZAF	02.05.45	12.10.45

SQUADRON USAGE

New Zealand's second fighter unit formed in the UK, on 3 March 1942, and Kirton in Lindsey was 486 Squadron's first base. The assigned CO, S/L C.L.C. Roberts, arrived a week later, followed rapidly by other pilots. While the CO was British, the two flight commanders, Flight Lieutenants J.G. Clouston and H.N. Sweetman were New Zealanders. The new squadron was originally equipped with Hawker Hurricanes for the night-fighting role, to work in collaboration with No. 1453 Flight, the Turbinlite unit equipped with Douglas Havoc/Boston aircraft (see *SQUADRONS! 24*). The first Hurricanes were soon taken on charge and training started on the 15th, a total of 269 hours and 20 minutes being flown by the end of March. By that time, the squadron was using a mixed force of Hurricane Mk.Is (V7719/J), Mk.IIAs (Z2803/T, Z4969/G, BV169/Z, BV172 and DG621/H) and Mk.IIBs (Z3434/L, Z3646/V, Z3684/N, Z3780/D, Z3914/R, Z5217/B, Z5220/F, Z5223/A, Z5258/P, Z5309/K, Z5333/U, Z5346/W, Z5470/S, BD728/X and BE161/Y). In April, night-flying practice began; the Hurricanes were re-painted dull black and long-range tanks removed while the squadron moved to Wittering. On 27 April, the first sorties were carried out, a dawn convoy patrol flown without incident by F/L Sweetman and P/O A.E. Umbers. Two nights later, the two flight commanders flew the first, albeit uneventful, joint patrol, with a Boston from 1453 Flight, 10 miles off the coast. It was not long before 486 lost its first Hurricane on operations. On 2 May,

One of the first Hurricane IIBs received by the squadron, Z5309/SA-K, still in daytime camouflage. (*via P. Sortehaug*)

One of the earliest groupings of 486 Squadron at Wittering, left to right.
Seating on wing: R.D. Fairbrother and K.K. Moore, both groundcrew.
Standing: P/O V.C. Fittall, P/O L.V. Weir (†31.10.42), K.G. Sgt Taylor-Cannon (†13.04.45 as OC 486), P/O A.E. Umbers (†14.02.45 as OC 486), S/L C.L.C. Roberts (British, CO), F/L H.N. Sweetman, Sgt G.E. Rawson (†24.10.43, 183 Sqn), Sgt N.E. Preston (†16.09.43), Sgt R.H. Fitzgibbon (†06.09.43), Sgt B.C. Thompson, P/O A.J. Woodgate.
Front: F/O T. Ness (Adjutant), Sgt H.C. Saward (PoW 24.09.43), F/Sgt G.G. Thomas (†09.04.43, CGS), Sgt C.N. Gall, Sgt F. Murphy, Sgt I.D. Waddy (PoW 25.08.44 as OC 164 Sqn), Sgt L. Walker, Sgt R.I. Philipps (†02.10.42) and Sgt R.J. Dall (†04.07.45, 33 Sqn). *(via P. Sortehaug)*

Sgt GE Rawson ran out of petrol and landed wheels up after dark. He was slightly injured, receiving cuts to his face and head, but the Hurricane was only good for scrap. A few days later, F/L Sweetman made a bad landing in bad visibility when returning from a patrol, damaging the Hurricane, although in this case it was eventually repaired. A similar accident occurred to Sgt C.N. Gall two weeks later. This was a rather high accident ratio considering only 25 sorties were performed in May. In June, the number of patrols increased to 86, helped by the fact that 486 dispatched three aircraft each night to Hibaldstow to operate with the Bostons of 1459 Flight. On 13 June, in a rare daytime sortie, F/L Clouston and P/O I.H. Irvine scrambled for aerodrome defence shortly after midday, but it was all for nothing. In July, the number of sorties was halved but more practice and exercises were flown. It was during an exercise that Irvine lost his life when he hit treetops and crashed just south-west of Sudbury. The squadron also experienced two other incidents during the month but without major consequence for pilots or aircraft. On the more positive side, 486 opened its scoreboard in July. During the night of 23/24 July, F/L Sweetman was flying a night patrol when he saw an aircraft flying northeast of Peterborough just below him; he soon identified it as a Do217 flying at 7,000 feet. While he saw the Dornier, the German gunners also saw him and opened fire; Sweetman promptly attacked the bomber. He fired a short burst at close range and saw the Dornier start a dive to evade. Sweetman followed and fired two more short bursts in quick succession from an astern quarter. The German aircraft then disappeared but, soon after, Sweetman saw an explosion, followed by a conflagration which quickly died down. It was later confirmed the Do217 had been downed near Fleet Fen, about 12 miles north-east of the town, but, after some jubilation over the squadron's first claim, Sweetman was disappointed to learn it had to be shared with a Canadian crew from No 409 Squadron who had filed a claim for the same aircraft.

Major changes were coming in July when the first Typhoons were taken on charge. It was intended at first to use the Typhoons at night. The first of them, R7766 and R7866, on 30 July. A week later, 13 had been taken on charge and training had begun, while operations continued for a little while on Hurricanes, the last sorties eventually being flown on 16 August. In all, 172 sorties were flown on Hurricanes. Nine days later, the first sorties were carried out with the Typhoons, a sea patrol flown by the CO and F/L Sweetman. When it became operational, 486 had Typhoons R7631, R7766, R7866/D, R8660/T, R8682/A, R8683/N, R8684/B, R8696, R8697/Z, R8698/QR8699/S, R8700/S, R8701/P, R8704/V, R8712/K and R8744/M on charge. A new chapter in 486's existence had begun. However, those first two sorties were a false start. Indeed, in September, no ops were carried out, the squadron continuing to focus on training, and over 450 hours were flown. It was soon discovered, however, that the Typhoon was too fast to fly with the Turbinlite aircraft; consequently, it was decided to switch 486 to the day-fighter role. Despite the change in role, the Kiwis did well with the Typhoon and in September no major incident was recorded. At the end of the month, 486 moved to West Malling. The true beginning of the Typhoon era took place on 2 October when the squadron, with No. 609 Squadron, participated in *Circus* 221, an escort for 12 Bostons bombing Le Havre's docks; 486 provided ten Typhoons led by the CO. A true start, but a bad one as well as, on return, the formation was intercepted by six Fw190s. The Fw190s remained at long range and didn't try to close, opening fire from afar. At first it was thought none of the aircraft had been hit but it was soon discovered that Pilot Officer RI Philips was flying at 200 feet, straight and level and obviously not at a safe speed; soon after, it was found he was not responding on the R/T. The Kiwis returned to base without Philips who was posted missing over the Channel. From that day, 486 was called upon regularly to provide escort or fly patrols. During one of these, on 17 October, they achieved their first success with the Typhoons. On a coastal patrol between Selsey Bill and Dungeness, P/O G.G. Thomas and Sgt A.N. Sames sighted two Fw190s a mile and a half ahead low down over the sea. The Germans dropped their bombs on Hastings and retreated south, splitting up in the process. Thomas and Sames pursued the 190 that took the more southerly route, the former firing several short bursts of fire which obliged the German to begin to take evasive action. The two New Zealanders managed to get closer, within 500 yards, where Thomas fired several more short bursts, hitting the aircraft in the fuselage and causing it to wing over and fly through Sames's line of cannon fire. The Fw190 straightened out at sea level and climbed slowly, enabling Sames to fire three additional short bursts, the last two of which hit both the fuselage and engine. That was the end of the Fw190 as it crashed into the sea a few seconds later. The claim was shared by the two pilots. Over 250 sorties were flown in October, but Philips would not be the only loss 486 sustained that month. On 16 October, Sgt D.B. Clark had his engine catch fire on patrol and crash landed safely near Battle. A few days later, F/Sgt Jesse Pearse also experienced trouble during a patrol and tried to bale out, but he became stuck in the cockpit and crashed with the aircraft near Ashford while, on the last day of the month, F/O L.V. Weir crashed off Selsey Bill for unknown reasons and was posted missing. Beside those operational losses, one more Typhoon was lost in an accident and, on the same day Weir was lost, P/O R.J. Dall overturned on landing at Tangmere; he was unhurt. In November, the squadron, now based at Tangmere, was limited to flying coastal patrols. The month was a quiet one if Sgt L Walker's engine failure during a practice flight and subsequent forced landing in a field near Durrington is ignored; Walker got away uninjured, but the Typhoon was wrecked. In December, close to 450 sorties were flown despite unfavourable weather. The Kiwis performed well, claiming no less than seven aircraft destroyed and another damaged between 17 and 24 December. These claims were all made during anti-Rhubarb patrols off the Selsey area. This improved performance came at a cost: Sgt R.W. Penny was thought to have been shot down by return fire from a Do217 he attacked with P/O Thomas (the latter eventually brought the German bomber down). While 1942 ended in an understandably satisfying way, 1943 started badly when Sgt PC Fisher was badly injured in a crash on landing when returning from a patrol. His airspeed indicator had failed during the flight and he was led in to land by F/O Dall. Fisher caught the slipstream of the leading aircraft, however, and crashed; the Typhoon caught immediately fire, but Fisher was extracted before it was too late. Otherwise, 486 beat its record by carrying out over 460 sorties in a month, adding one Bf109 destroyed on the 17th (Sgt K.C. Taylor-Cannon). Operational activity increased in the next two months, with 490 sorties flown in February and 690 in March. The mission given to the Kiwis remained unchanged – anti-Rhubarb patrols. Flying so many patrols increased the chances of intercepting German fighter-bombers and

Two Hurricanes, painted now in Night camouflage, Z3353/SA-M and BD725/SA-J about to taxi for a night patrol. (*via P. Sortehaug*)

The squadron was soon re-equipped with Hawker Typhoons, the first ones having the undersurfaces painted in Night for night operations like this one R8697/SA-Z.
(*via P. Sortehaug*)

some successes were filed in February and March. On 8 February, F/L Sweetman and Sgt Walker managed to intercept four Fw190s and damage one each while, one week later, F/Sgt Frank Murphy got a reconnaissance Ju88. In March, an Fw190 was shot down on the 1st by F/Sgt W.B. Tyerman and another was claimed as destroyed on the 14th by F/Sgt R.H. Fitzgibbon; owing to the length of the chase, he ran out of petrol and made a forced landing near Tarring Neville, sealing the fate of the Typhoon and cancelling out, in a way, the destruction of the Fw190. On the debit side, besides Fitzgibbon's aircraft on the 14th, 486 suffered some losses during those two months. On 24 February, Fitzgibbon and F/Sgt R.E. Preston crashed on take-off. Fitzgibbon had one of his tyres burst and he lost control; Preston, who was his wingman, attempted to avoid him by 'hopping' his Typhoon but eventually stalled as he was not going fast enough. Fortunately, the misadventure ended well for the two pilots but both aircraft were struck off charge. March saw three Typhoons written off. The other mishaps took place on the 1st during an engagement, at the end of which one Fw190 was destroyed, when F/Sgt M.O. Jorgenson got water in his air intake and was compelled to make a forced landing at Selsey Bill; on the 24th, F/Sgt W.K. Mawson was posted missing on a Rhubarb over the Continent after being hit by flak in the Étretat–Fécamp area (one of the very few Rhubarbs carried out during this period). It was later learned he had become a PoW after making a forced landing. His Typhoon was repaired and tested by the Germans.

A new era began on 1 April with a change of command. Squadron Leader D.J. Scott, a New Zealander, was posted from No. 198 Squadron to command, while S/L Roberts was posted to No. 257 Squadron as CO. The new commander started very well, sharing in the probable destruction of an Fw190 over Étretat on 9 April and claiming another as damaged. A few days later, S/L Scott performed once more when, 20 miles north-west of St Aubin, he managed to bag a Bf109 with F/Sgt Fitzgibbon, a claimed again shared by the two pilots. Two days later, a rare claim was made with a Bf109 credited destroyed to the squadron and not specific pilots. That happened during a dogfight near Le Havre when the squadron was flying on a Ramrod, escorting Typhoon fighter-bombers of No 181 Squadron; the Bf109, which was attacking P/O Gall, was caught by Gall's slipstream and span in to ground. Then, on 29 April, P/O Murphy and F/O A.H. Smith destroyed a Bf109 south of the Isle of Wight during an anti-Rhubarb patrol. April proved a very positive month as only one Typhoon was wrecked when, on 16 April, F/L Sweetman experienced engine trouble and was forced to make for land near Selsey; he escaped unhurt. May was more balanced, 486 sustaining two losses and one pilot killed (F/O AA Brown was shot down by flak off Le Havre during a shipping recce on the 16th). Later in the month, F/Sgt D Bennett experienced engine trouble during *Ramrod* 80 and was obliged to make a forced landing near Saint Helens on the Isle of Wight. Against those losses, only one claim was made: an Fw190 destroyed south of Brighton by the CO. In May, the number of sorties was cut by a third compared to April and, in June, 486 flew a third less sorties again, so just under 200. The squadron recorded no loss, but its scoreboard increased with two more Fw190s destroyed, both shot down on the 24th near the mouth of the Somme and credited to the CO and F/L A.E. Umbers. July was also free of loss, while the level of operational activity was maintained. Only one engagement took place, which ended with two more Fw190s destroyed and two more probably destroyed. That occurred on 15 July while carrying out an air–sea rescue over the Channel for a downed Wellington. The Fw190s engaged the protective Typhoons, but it soon turned to the advantage of the Kiwis. One confirmed victory was shared between the CO and F/Sgt Fitzgibbon, while P/O Sames was credited with a second; F/L Umbers and P/O Murphy each claimed an Fw190 damaged. However, in light of the reports made on return, Umbers and Murphy later had their claims upgraded to probably destroyed. Excluding the ground collision on the 3rd between F/O Gall and Sgt JR Powell while taxiing for another operational sortie, August was rather uneventful.

In September, 486 continued to fly escorts, Roadstead and Ramrods, and sometimes sweeps over northern France and Belgium, most of the time as part of the wing. Few encounters with German fighters were made and the number of claims reflected this, being limited to two Fw190s damaged (the CO and F/L Umbers) on the 24th but for the cost of F/Sgt H.C. Saward who was shot down by the 190s and became a PoW. The next day, S/L Scott left the squadron with a DSO and a promotion to wing commander to become wing leader of the Tangmere Wing. He was replaced by F/L I.D. Waddy. This was at the end of what had proved to be a bad month for the Kiwis. On the 16th, Pilot Officer N.E. Preston and Flight Sergeants M.O. Jorgensen and D Bennet were all shot down and

Typhoon JP532/SA-T seen soon after its delivery to 486 Squadron at Tangmere in July 1943. It was one of the last Typhoons produced before the interim canopy improvements took place. (*CT Collection*)

killed by flak near Le Havre during a Roadstead over Dieppe–Le Havre. This was a severe setback for the Kiwis who had, to date, managed to limit their losses. This was the worst loss sustained since formation. Until the end of the year, 486 was airborne another 600 times, did not add to its score, but suffered further losses. Two were in October: F/Sgt C.J. Sheddan was hit by flak on the 1st, ditched into the Channel and spent 19 hours in a dinghy before being rescued; on the 9th, F/Sgt K McCarthy crashed on landing in bad visibility at Lympne while ferrying an aircraft to the station. In November, P/O W.B. Tyerman was shot down and killed by flak near Dunkirk during a night-intruder sortie on the 10th, and F/Sgt N.E.A. Helean suffered an engine failure during a test flight on the 20th. These incidents do not include two other Typhoons destroyed when a Halifax crashed while trying to land at Tangmere. In December, F/Sgt Helean was lost on the 21st (cause uncertain, engine failure or flak) but evaded capture, becoming the squadron's first evader. He was reported safe in September 1944. Less lucky was F/O R.A. Peters who was posted missing from operations after he had to ditch his Typhoon in the Channel off New Haven; he was never seen again.

In January 1944, the squadron managed to carry out more than 220 sorties, most achieved under the new CO, S/L J.H. Iremonger, a British officer, who took over on the 7th; Waddy, a founding member of the squadron, was tour-expired. Still flying the same operational sorties, 486 suffered a single loss that month when F/O G Philp was shot down and killed south of Paris on the 14th during a long-range sweep. The same day, three Tempests were received for familiarisation purposes (JN733/X, JN735/Y and JN738/Z). They were followed by two more on the 21st, JN739/W and JN743/V, while operational duties continued with the Typhoons. The aim was to create a Tempest Wing with Nos 3 and 56 Squadrons. That seems to have been premature as, at the end of February, 486 made another move, this time to Drem (the squadron had moved to Beaulieu to operate in the Middle Wallop sector at the end of January), leaving its Tempests to 3 Squadron, owing to a lack of aircraft, and continued to fly the Typhoon.

In the meantime, on the last day of January, 486 moved to Beaulieu to operate from Middle Wallop with its Typhoons, causing a drop in sorties completed during the following weeks (resulting in less than 100 for February). As in January, February saw one pilot lost; F/Sgt W.J. Swinton became a PoW on the 10th after his aircraft was hit by flak on a sweep near Melun. At the end of the month, 486 made another move, being incorporated into No. 148 Airfield at Drem as part of the Turnhouse Sector. The winds of change had arrived again, however. In March, 486 transferred to No. 149 Airfield at Castle Camp. With an Armament Practice Camp carried out later in the month, the number of operational sorties was a mere eight in March with a single op, a convoy patrol, flown on the 5th. On the 13th, during a non-operational flight, W/O H.K. Williams was killed when he suffered an engine failure and crashed south of Downham. Taken to hospital with severe burns, he died during the night. Three weeks later, another Kiwi pilot was killed in an accident when his Typhoon spun in at night near Croxton. In April, a few sorties were carried out, the last ones,

ASR sorties, on the 14th making for a grand total of over 5,260 sorties on the Typhoon, a record for a Typhoon unit. The Typhoon era was at its end, however, as, at the close of April, 486 transferred to No. 150 Airfield at Newchurch where the final conversion to Tempests took place. Indeed, in April, the squadron converted for good; the first Tempest of the new batch arrived early in the month following an Armament Practice Camp at Ayr, the squadron being temporarily based at Castle Camps. Conversion consumed the month and, on the 29th, 486 moved to Newchurch, midway between Hastings and Dover, with its sixteen Tempests where it joined 3 Squadron (now fully equipped with the new aircraft). The third squadron of 150 Airfield (renamed 150 Wing in May), 56, was still flying the Typhoon; its conversion occurred in June. Two days before the move, 486 lost its first Tempest when, after an engine failure during a practice flight, F/O H.M. Mason was obliged to make a forced landing at Castle Camps, wrecking the aircraft in the process; he escaped unscathed. Now based at Newchurch, the first Tempest sorties were carried out on 1 May. Flying Officers J.G. Wilson and W.A. Hart went on patrol off Dungeness, but the flight ended badly for Wilson. His engine over-speeded and he had to make the unit's second forced landing in four days, crashing near Staple where the Tempest broke into several pieces. The aircraft was too damaged to repair, but Wilson was unhurt. Other patrols were flown the next day and, on the 3rd, the first offensive sweep was carried out. Eight Tempests led by the CO took off at 14.05, joining nine aircraft of 3 Squadron for *Ramrod* 826. It was a fighter sweep over the north-east of France in connection with a series of bombing raids by medium bombers. The engines continued to give trouble as the CO was obliged to return early, leaving F/L H.N. Sweetman to lead for the rest of the uneventful op. Over the next few days, 486 flew various patrols or shipping recces, and, more rarely, some Rangers or Ramrods (each involving several aircraft). More important assignments were also completed with a Roadstead on the 18th, two fighter sweeps in the Lille area on the 19th and 20th, and another sweep over Cambrai on the 24th. Two more ops were flown on the 29th near the Berck–Saint-Pol and Furnes–Lille areas but, excluding some targets of opportunity, May was simply uneventful despite 180 operational sorties being flown.

The first days of June continued the trend with only a handful of patrols or shipping recces carried out. On D-Day, the squadron was kept in reserve at full readiness all day and was ultimately not required, except for routine shipping/weather recces and shipping patrols, until dusk when elements of the wing patrolled the Bay of Seine and landed at Ford. The next day, several scrambles were carried out, but all interceptions proved friendly. On the 8th, however, 486 and 3 Squadrons went on the offensive for the first time since D-Day with a sweep performed in the Caen area just after midday. Some Bf109s were sighted and attacked by W/C R.P. Beamont and 3 Squadron while 486 remained as top cover. Later in the afternoon, another sweep was ordered near the Fécamp–Amiens area but was cancelled before the aircraft reached the French coast owing to adverse weather. Two days later, the 10th, was also a busy day with sweeps and patrols carried out but luck was not on the squadron's side as, on the first sweep (targeting Le Havre), a Tempest was attacked by a Spitfire; fortunately, the attacker broke off before it was too late. On the second sweep of the day, which took place late in the evening, the Tempest flown by P/O F.B. Lawless, while heading for Caen, developed engine trouble to the point he had to ditch in the Channel. Fortunately, he was only slightly injured and was soon picked up by an ASR launch. That was the first ditching made by a Tempest. The rest of the formation continued on and F/L W.L. Miller was later caught by flak; his aircraft was damaged badly enough to necessitate a safe forced landing at Ford. The Tempest was soon repaired. During the

Tempest JN738/SA-Z, one of the first issued to 486 Sqn in January 1944. It was transferred to 3 Sqn in February.

S/L Iremonger standing on Tempest JN763/SA-F in June 1944. *(CT Collection)*

next few days, 486 flew ops every day but all proved uneventful. A major event soon changed the unit's fate. The German V-1 had been introduced into combat and the first of them passed over before midnight on the 13th. This new threat had to be stopped and Air Defence Great Britain (formerly Fighter Command) switched to anti-Diver patrols, calling on the Tempest Wing to intercept the flying bombs. The first such patrols for 486 were carried out on the 16th; 44 were flown that day and the first V-1s spotted and destroyed. The very first one was credited to F/Sgt B.J. O'Connor who shot it down around midday between Rye and Dungeness. Forty minutes later, P/O K. McCarthy shot one down north of Rye, the V-1 exploding on the ground. The Tempest soon proved a remarkable tool in the V-1 hunt, especially in Kiwi hands, 486 scoring every day until the end of the month. Two were destroyed on the 17th, twelve on the 18th. The best day would be the 23rd with sixteen claims filed. For June alone, close to 100 V-1s were destroyed by the Kiwis. With such a scoreboard, some pilots soon became V-1 aces, like F/O Ray Cammock with 8.5, F/O Owen 'Ginger' Eagleson with eight, P/O 'Dan' Danzey with seven, Pilot Officers McCarthy and 'Black Mac' McCaw with six each, and F/O 'Bev' Hall and F/Sgt 'Sid' Short with five each. The Kiwis flew close to 800 sorties that month, but, despite appearances, it was far from a walk in the park. The squadron did not make it through the month unscathed. On the 22nd, F/O T.M. Fenton ran out of fuel on patrol and crashed at Newchurch; the aircraft was only good for scrap. The 28th was a really bad day. Late at night, F/O S.S. Williams and F/Sgt W.T. Wright were on patrol when they spotted and attacked a V-1; the attack was not decisive. Wright, however, was hit by friendly anti-aircraft fire. He was last heard to say he had been fired on and that he had been hit and was going to attempt a forced landing. He finally crashed into the sea off Beachy Head. Williams's aircraft was also hit but returned to base. Earlier that day, Lawless crashed in the vicinity of Rye after flying through a V-1 that exploded after he opened fire. Two days later, it was the turn of 'Sid' Short to see his Tempest damaged by debris from a V-1 he had just shot down; he crashed at the end of the runway, sealing the fate of his aircraft.

In July, the V-1 campaign continued and 486 beat another record by achieving close to 900 sorties. That month, 115 V-1s were destroyed by the Kiwis and new names appeared on the aces list (Flying Officers J.R. Cullen, W.A. Hart, G.J.M. Hooper, and W.A. Kalka, Pilot Officers F.B. Lawless, W.L. Miller and B.J. O'Connor, W/O C.J. 'Jimmy' Sheddan, and F/O S.S. Williams) while the June aces continued to increase their tallies. This impressive record had a high cost. On 1 July, P/O K. McCarthy crashed in a wood near Hastings after an engine failure during an anti-Diver patrol. He was seriously injured. On 3 July, Miller baled out of his Tempest after the engine failed during a night patrol, the visibility being too poor to consider a forced landing. The next day, Williams crashed when his undercarriage refused to deploy upon returning from a night patrol. He was unhurt but the Tempest could not be repaired. The next day, Sheddan, after destroying two V-1s, started to attack a third when a spent shell hit his air intake. The Tempest was wrecked in the forced landing at Netherfield and Sheddan seriously injured. After several days without major incident, 486 began another bad run of luck. On the 20th, W/O S.J. Short was fired on by Allied flak during a patrol and his engine hit. He crashed at Deanland, emerging unhurt from a machine too damaged to repair. Then, in two days, the squadron lost three Tempests. The first, on the 23rd, was lost when P/O W.A.L. Trott returned to base with engine trouble after destroying two V-1s. He made a forced landing at Stonecross. The Tempest did not survive the crash, but Trott was unhurt. Then, the next day, Kalka

Tempests JN754/SA-A and JN801/SA-L in full D-Day markings at Newchurch during the early stages of the V-1 campaign. Below, the left side of S/L Iremonger's JN763/SA-F in June 1944. The squadron leader pennant was only worn on the left side. *(CT Collection)*

and F/L N.J. Powell suffered the same misadventure when engine failures led to forced landings (six miles north of Friston for Kalka and near Snargate for Powell). Both pilots were safe, but their Tempests were wrecked. Flight Lieutenant E.W. Tanner's aircraft suffered the same fate when its brakes seized on landing at Newchurch. Worse was to come as, on the last day of the month during a patrol, F/Sgt A.A .Wilson collided near Brexhill with a Spitfire XIV from 91 Squadron. Both pilots were killed. Forty-five more V-1s were claimed in August, the last on 31 August by O'Connor. At the end of the hunt, the top scorers were Eagleson with 21, followed by Cammock with 20.5; four more pilots scored ten V-1s or more. Three Tempests were written off in August however. The first was flown by Ray Cammock on the 10th; just after take-off, he experienced an engine failure and subsequently made a forced landing at south west of Battle. He was safe, but the same could not be said for F/Sgt J.W. Waddell who crashed during an anti-Diver patrol on the 17th. The Tempest crashed into high ground near Tenterden, killing Waddell instantly. The real circumstances of the crash were never established but it seems that the poor visibility was responsible. While the last V-1 was destroyed on 31 August, 486 continued to fly anti-Diver patrols until 4 September. It then switched back to the more aggressive task of fighter sweeps, escorts and seeking out V-2 sites. September was uneventful until the 19th when the wing moved to Matlask in anticipation of another move, this time to the Continent; for this reason the wing was placed under 2TAF command on the 28th. This move was part of the reorganisation of 2TAF, the Tempest Wing replacing the Mustangs of No. 122 Wing, which was recalled to the UK. The squadron was based at B.60/Grimbergen in Belgium with 3 and 56; the Tempest squadrons became the new flying units of 122 Wing. Wing Commander Beamont made the move too and remained wing leader. The CO was G/C P.G. Jameson, a New Zealand ace, who had had an eventful war having survived the Norwegian campaign, the sinking of HMS *Glorious*, the Battle of Britain, and Dieppe. Patrols and armed recces began immediately, especially in the Arnhem area where the British had recently launched an airborne operation. It would not be long before the Luftwaffe was encountered and the first kills recorded. On 30 September, F/L Williams was leading a patrol in the Arnhem area at 5000 feet when he spotted a single Bf109 flying east at 200/300 feet. He immediately reported to the top cover leader that he was going down to attack with his section. Williams broke formation and the Bf109 turned towards him, climbing slightly. Williams tried to get behind it but lost height in the process. He made various steep turns, still at about 200 feet above the Bf109, but it kept turning in to him until he was in a good position for a two-second burst with 95° deflection from about 600 yards. No strikes were seen and the Bf109 briefly disappeared from view. The German re-appeared from under the Tempest's nose, no longer turning, but climbing slightly and emitting glycol from its starboard radiator; the engine burst into flames. The Bf109 lost height and the pilot baled out at about 400/500 feet just before his aircraft crashed into a wood and blew up. This was the squadron's first confirmed kill of a manned aircraft since its conversion to the Tempest.

On 1 October, the squadron moved with the wing to B.80/Volkel in the Netherlands from where it continued armed recces and

486 Squadron posing at the height of the V-1 campaign in July 1944:
On the fuselage, left to right: W/O O.D. Eagleson, W/O A.H. Bailey (†26.03.45), F/O H.M. Mason, Pilot Officers W.A.L. Trott and F.B. Lawless, F/L J.H. McCaw, W/O J.H. Stafford, F/L L.J. Appleton and F/Sgt H.N. Steedman.
On the wing, left to right: F/Sgt J.W. Waddell (†17.08.44), and Flying Officers S.S. Williams (†22.12.44) and F/O R.J. Cammock (†06.10.44).
On the box: Pilot Officers J.G. Wilson and R.D. Bremner.
Standing, left to right: Flying Officers W.H. Cole (Adj, British) and W.J.H. Sayers (MO, British), Flight Lieutenants J.R. Cullen (PoW 04.05.45) and V.StC. Cooke, P/O B.M. Hall (†27.12.44), S/L J.H. Iremonger (CO), Flying Officers W.A. Hart (PoW 07.10.44) and R.J. Danzey, and Flight Lieutenants E.W. Tanner and H.N. Sweetman. Kneeling: F/O W.L. Miller and W/O W.A. Kalka (†25.03.45). *(JR Cullen via P. Sortehaug)*

Tempest NV753/SA-J was issued to 486 Sqn in February 1945. It was mainly flown by P/O W.J. Shaw during the final weeks of the war. Shaw made his last claims flying this aircraft.

patrols, which proved to be full of danger. The first half of the month was difficult. On the 1st, two aircraft experienced engine trouble. While F/L K.G. Taylor-Cannon managed to get back home, P/O B.M. Hall had to make a forced landing just short of base, fortunately without major consequences for him or his aircraft. A few days later, on the 6th, during the course of an armed recce northeast of Arnhem, a goods train and about twenty trucks were attacked. Flight Lieutenant Cammock was hit by flak fired from the surrounding area. While at 500 feet, his engine caught fire and the Tempest ploughed directly into the rear of the train; Cammock was probably killed in the crash. The next day, F/O W.A. Hart was also hit while attacking a goods train south-east of Wesel. Luck was with him, however, as his engine only seized and, as he was flying at 2000 feet, he was high enough to bale out successfully, albeit straight into German hands. Returning from the same attack, W/O W.A. Bailey's engine started giving him trouble and he made a forced landing at Langstraat, in the vicinity of Volkel. He was soon back at base but the Tempest was eventually struck off charge owing to the considerable damage it sustained. Another Tempest was hit by flak three days later, but F/L E.W. Tanner managed to save himself and the aircraft with a nice forced landing near the Nijmegen bridge. The next day, the wing suffered a body blow when the wing leader, W/C R.P. Beamont was shot down and made a PoW. He was replaced by W/C J.B. Wray. Things calmed down after that, even though further engine troubles were reported, and the situation remained stable until the end of the month with about 350 sorties carried out. Aerial encounters were rare even though some sightings were made, including of the latest German threat, the Me262, a jet aircraft. On the 28th, luck was on 486's side. Late in the afternoon, some Me262s were observed approaching base from the south. Two were attacked with no obvious results by F/O R.J. Danzey who was returning home alone with a duff engine; he came across another five and managed to hit one from extreme range. He was then forced to break off when threatened from the rear. The Me262 was credited as damaged.

The rhythm of operations was maintained in November. No loss was recorded, but the squadron's scoreboard increased. On the 19th, while on standing patrol, the formation was in the Rheine area when two Me262s were seen preparing for take-off from Rheine aerodrome. Led by F/L Taylor-Cannon, the Tempests dived and strafed the two jets, Taylor-Cannon and Eagleson probably destroying one while the second was claimed as damaged on the ground by P/O J. Steedman. Flight Lieutenant Taylor-Cannon would again be in the spotlight a few days later. On an early morning patrol, two Ju188s were encountered over an airfield to the east of Münster. One was just in the landing pattern, but the other appeared to be having some difficulty getting its undercarriage down. Flight Lieutenants Taylor-Cannon and Williams both fired on the latter and appeared to have hit the pilot for the aircraft pulled up vertically, blazing end to end; it was then seen to explode and a single parachute open. Steedman attacked the other Ju188, seeing strikes in the cockpit area, whereupon the aircraft collided with a tree, which was knocked over. The bomber then skidded along the ground, leaving a long furrow. The first Ju188 was credited as destroyed, and shared by the two pilots, but the second one, although initially claimed as destroyed, ultimately, and somewhat bizarrely, was only credited as a probable. Because of non-favourable weather, the number of sorties dropped to 250 in December, a month which also saw a change of command; S/L Iremonger was posted out on the 11th, tour expired. He was replaced by F/L A.E. Umbers from 3 Squadron. The first three weeks of the month were uneventful until F/L S. Williams was shot down and killed by flak near Vreden during a Ranger on the 22nd. He was avenged on Christmas Day. While flying a patrol in the Julich–Malmedy area, the squadron, led by the CO, was flying south of Aachen at 10,000 feet when, an hour into the flight, F/O J.H. Stafford and P/O P.D. Bremner spotted a Me262 at 11,000 feet flying west at 1500 yards range. The squadron climbed, but Stafford lost it in the sun; the Me262 soon came out of sun travelling north at high speed; Stafford broke up towards him and commenced firing at extreme range, continuing into 400 yards. He saw pieces fall away from the left nacelle. As the Me262 passed over, several red balls fell from it and the aircraft slowed considerably. Stafford got in behind as it started a moderate turn to the left. He closed the Me262 to 600 yards and fired again. The jet straightened out of the turn as he fired and dived, leaving a trail of white smoke. The Me262 rapidly built up speed and Stafford chased, firing occasional bursts. The jet pulled up and did a slow roll, straightening out as Stafford fired again. The Me262 then rolled on its back and Stafford saw the pilot bale out; the parachute did not open properly. The Me262 crashed and exploded seven miles from Aachen. Stafford was accompanied throughout the engagement by Bremner who also managed to fire at the Me262. For this reason, the Me262 was shared between the two Kiwis. The next day saw a collision between two aircraft, one flown by F/O C.J. MacDonald and the other by P/O B.J. O'Connor. That happened during another patrol of the same area as the day before. Once more, an Me262 was sighted and, in the hurry to get at it, the two Tempests clipped one another. Luck was with the Kiwis as no one was hurt; MacDonald parachuted to safety and O'Connor made a forced landing in the American lines. The following day, a major encounter for 2TAF took place. It all began with several armed recces over the Paderborn area around midday. Another Tempest squadron had already shot down four Fw190s when 486 arrived on the scene. The Kiwis were made aware by the controller that enemy aircraft were in the vicinity. Indeed, the squadron was soon under attack by about forty Fw190 and Bf109s. A furious dogfight ensued, a real challenge because it was soon discovered the Fw190s were the latest long-nose versions, but the Kiwis eventually got the advantage. Flight Lieutenants Tanner and Taylor-Cannon each claimed one Fw190 shot down as did F/O K.A. Smith and P/O S.J. Short. Two more claims were also credited to Tanner and F/O B.M. Hall for a Bf109 probably destroyed and another damaged

Volkel, during the winter of 1944–45, showing Tempests of 486 Sqn taxiing out for their next sortie over Germany.
Above, NV937/SA-C stayed with 486 for just two weeks. After striking trees near Paderborn, the Tempest left the squadron for repairs and never returned.
(KA Smith via P. Sortehaug)

Volkel, during the winter of 1944–45, showing Tempests of 486 Sqn taxiing out for their next sortie over Germany. Below, NV988/SA-Y was shot down on 15 April 1945. The pilot, F/O R.E. Evans, survived. *(KA Smith via P. Sortehaug)*

respectively. The latter made his claim just before being shot down and killed by Fw190s.

The Luftwaffe attacked various Allied airfields on 1 January 1945. An armed recce led by the CO was already in the air when they were recalled at Arnhem to mix it up with the Luftwaffe over the Eindhoven area. They dropped their extra fuel tanks and the formation of eight Tempests rushed toward the town. Three Fw190s were sighted, two at 6000 feet and the one very low flying north towards Helmond. The Tempests split up and S/L Umbers chose the 190 on the deck. He opened fire from 300 yards and saw immediate strikes on the wing roots and fuselage. Black and white smoke streamed back from the Fw190 as it dramatically slowed down, forcing Umbers to pull up violently to avoid a collision. The fate of the Fw190 was sealed and Umbers was able to watch it crash and burst into flames. Immediately after, he saw a solitary Bf109 about a mile away flying east at 1500 feet. The German pilot spotted the two Tempests, immediately dived to ground level and attempted to join a gaggle of twenty other Bf109s in the vicinity. Umbers opened fire just as the pilot turned but saw no hits. The Bf109 straightened out with the main formation which then broke violently. Umbers was able to follow and, when the German straightened out, fired a short burst from 100 yards, obtaining hits on the cockpit, right wing root and fuselage. The Bf109's right wheel dropped, its speed fell off and, as it began to disappear under the Tempest's nose, Umbers saw the aircraft hit the ground and explode. The CO was not the only one to score that morning; P/O C.J. Sheddan claimed one Fw190 destroyed, F/O W.A.L. Trott and P/O G.J.M. Hooper claimed an Fw190 destroyed and Bf109 damaged each, while P/O J. Steedman claimed an Fw190 as damaged. The Kiwis suffered no loss. While the Luftwaffe had attempted to neutralise 2TAF and the US Ninth Air Force for a while, the operation failed, Allied losses being quickly replaced, something the Germans could not do as easily. The routine of ops returned in the hours following the attack. The squadron flew various armed recces over the next few days, the weather preventing much flying, but the Kiwis scored against targets of opportunity. On the 13th, 486 was flying an armed recce in the Saint Vith area when they were fired on by mistake by American anti-aircraft batteries near Euskirchen. The flak was accurate and three Tempests were hit badly enough to abruptly end their flight. The CO crashed near Verviers in the American lines, while P/O W. Kalka had to evacuate his aircraft. Flight Lieutenant L.J. Appleton made a forced landing near Euskirchen, seriously wounded in the neck and face. He was initially posted missing and it would take a fortnight to determine his fate when he was transferred to the 8th British General Hospital in Brussels. His war was over and, upon recovery, he was sent home. Two other Tempests were also hit but the pilots succeeded in returning to base. Despite this bad experience, the squadron was up again the next day for another armed recce, this time over the Paderborn area. Around midday, a Bf109 and Fw190 were sighted flying low, three miles north of Münster. The Tempests went after them immediately. The Bf109 was attacked by F/O C.J. McDonald and shot down. A couple of minutes later, two more Bf109s and an Fw190 were sighted flying north-west at ground level, three miles west of Münster this time. They were engaged and the fate of one Fw190 was sealed by W/O J.E. Wood. These two claims helped to calm the anger of the previous day. With the weather improving, more sorties were flown and, consequently, there were more opportunities to encounter the Luftwaffe. January 23 proved to be a fruitful day for 122 Wing which claimed 22 aircraft shot down, not counting targets on the ground destroyed or damaged. From this total, 486 contributed two Bf109s destroyed, one Fw190 probably destroyed, and two Fw190s and a Bf109 damaged. The victorious pilots were S/L A.E. Umbers, who was credited with one Bf109 shot down near Rheine, while the second Bf109 was shared between by F/O J.H. Stafford and W/O A.H. Bailey, and a third Bf109 was claimed as damaged by W/O W.J. Campbell around 16.05. On a previous armed recce, which had taken place between 12.20 and 14.05, some Fw190s had been engaged, leading to the probable destruction of a Fw190 in the Minden area by F/O R.J. Danzey, while three more Fw190s had been also claimed as damaged by F/L W.L. Miller and F/O R.D. Bremner.

After close to 200 sorties in January, 486 didn't do much better in February, flying just twenty more, but its scoreboard continued to grow. The first claim was recorded on the 2nd. The day had started badly, however, as, during a morning armed recce, P/O G.J.M. Hooper was shot down while attacking a stationary loco five miles south-west of Nienburg. Hit, he called on the radio to say he was okay and about to attempt a landing, which he did successfully. He was captured the next day. Hooper would eventually manage to escape and evade two months later, crossing the US lines on 19 April. Soon after midday, his loss was balanced with the interception of a Do217 on approach to the airstrip at Paderborn. It was first sighted by Bremner who was followed by Stafford and Sheddan. Bremner opened fire from 800 yards just as the Dornier was touching down. He saw strikes on the wing roots and cockpit, and the Do217 swerved to the left. Bremner pulled up and was able to see flames on the side of the aircraft. The Dornier was finished off by Stafford and Sheddan, coming to a stop and exploding. The claim was shared by the three pilots. The next day, Stafford, helped this time by Eagleson, caught two Ju52s hidden in woods south of Hanover and damaged both. Then, the squadron lost two Tempests in a week, F/L W.L. Miller on the 8th near Verden and Arthur Umbers on the 14th near Meppen. Both were shot down while attacking ground targets, Miller hit by debris, Umbers by flak. Miller was lucky and was rescued by the Dutch resistance, remaining hidden until the Canadians liberated the zone two months later. The CO, sadly, was killed; attacking barges, he was caught under intense rocket flak. His Tempest was immediately boxed in, flicked over on its back and dived directly into the canal in flames. It was a bad day for the Kiwis who had already seen the departure of another pilot, F/O W.A.L. Trott. Also hit by flak, but injured by shrapnel in the lower abdomen, he managed to make it home where he landed his Tempest. He recovered from his wounds but his war was over. A new CO was promoted the next day, Keith Taylor-Cannon, B Flight being taken over by Neville Powell. The second fortnight of the month came down on 486's side. On the 22nd, two Bf109s were shot down near Münster. The two victorious pilots were Stafford and F/O A.R. Evans. Two days later, the new CO and Powell sealed the fate of two others near Bramsche, but the month ended with another loss the next day when W/O RC McPherson experienced engine trouble during an armed recce and made a forced landing in enemy territory. He was captured.

Tempest NV986/SA-F (S/L Taylor-Cannon' regular mount) about to start its engine in March 1945; a lucky photo as this aircraft only served three weeks that month as it was sent out for repairs after P/O Melles damaged the mainplane flying too low over the Dümmer See area.

Some of 486 Squadron's pilots after an op in March 1945. Left to right: Flying Officers O.D. Eagleson and D.J. Thomson, S/L K.G. Taylor-Cannon (CO, †17.04.45), F/O R.J. Danzey, W/O W.J. Shaw, F/L J.H. Stafford, and Flying Officers K.A. Smith (PoW 26.04.45), R.D. Bremner, C.J. MacDonald and A.R. Evans. All but Thomson and Shaw were awarded the DFC while serving with 486. *(KA Smith via P. Sortehaug)*

Close to 350 sorties were flown in March, thanks to the weather which made it possible to fly more often. Despite this, there were no encounters with the Luftwaffe. The squadron continued its armed recces and, until the 25th, did not record any loss. That day, F/O W.A. Kalka was hit by small arms fire near Vreden. While he was able to return to base, he was unable to land his Tempest owing to damage sustained to his ailerons. He baled out successfully but came down in the Maas River and drowned. Pilot Officer A.H. Bailey died the next day. He was hit by intense light flak near Gütersloh but made it a good way home, losing height as he went. His engine soon seized but he managed to stretch the glide across the Rhine. He made a forced landing in a field near Wesel but, in the failing light, ploughed into a stone house. A British Army ambulance was promptly on the scene and took him to a nearby hospital, but Bailey died on the way.

By April, German forces were collapsing everywhere. The Allies put on maximum pressure to accelerate the end. Therefore, more sorties were carried out, over 500 for 486. While March was free of any claims, April proved a very productive month with more than thirty made. The first two of the month were claimed by Sheddan on the 6th. In the early evening, he was part of a patrol of four Tempests near the Dümmer See–Steinhuder Meer area when, at around 20.00, they were advised by a forward contact car that Ju87s were attacking the bridge over the Weser at Stolzenau. Guided by AA fire, F/O C.J. Sheddan selected a Ju87 flying at about 4000 feet. He opened fire from 200 yards and closed to almost point-blank range. The Junkers was mortally hit and Sheddan had to manoeuvre violently to the left to avoid ramming it. Two parachutes were seen descending from the Junkers. There was no time to see what happened to them as Sheddan was now after a second dive-bomber which was about a mile from him. An easy prey, Sheddan closed in and opened fire once more from 200 yards, closing with three short bursts to 100 yards, but initially seeing no strikes. He pulled out to the left and made a further attack from the right. While positioning for a fourth attack, he saw a parachute open and the Ju87 commence a gliding turn. It spiralled slowly toward the ground and, soon after a second parachute opened, crashed and blew up. Four days later, in the evening during an armed recce, F/L W.E. Schrader claimed a Fw190 flying alone with long-range tanks at 8000 feet near Nienburg. This would be the last claim made from Volkel, the squadron moving to B.118/Hapsten in Germany two days later. Having been there for just a couple of hours, patrols and armed recces resumed and it was not long before another claim was made, this time by F/L J.H. Stafford who claimed a Fw190 destroyed east of Ludwigslust late in the evening. These claims were rapidly balanced by the loss of the CO and F/Sgt W.J.K. Hart. Having taken off on a late morning patrol to strafe motorised transport near Dömitz, almost over the bridge itself, the Tempest flown by S/L Taylor-Cannon was seen to suffer a direct hit from an 88 shell and catch fire. He baled out and was seen to land safely. Everyone could only hope he became a PoW, but no trace of him was ever found. What happened to him remains a mystery, but it is likely he was killed soon after he reached the ground. Neither his body nor his gravesite have been found. In the afternoon, Hart was in trouble. After having strafed METs and a loco, the patrol returned to base, but Hart's engine failed and he was forced to land at high speed in a small paddock near Rheine in British-held territory; things went wrong and he was badly injured in the process. He was recovered and spent the next few weeks in hospital before returning to the squadron in July; the war was over. The Kiwis got soon their revenge. The very next day, Sheddan shot down an Fw190 north of Ludwigslust in the middle of the afternoon and, in the evening, W/O W.J. Shaw claimed another while F/O S.J. Short claimed a Bf109 as damaged in the same area. The action started when the Tempests were caught by surprise while strafing along the rail tracks near Ludwigslust. Warrant Officer O.J. Mitchell was shot down and killed but Shaw managed to reverse the situation by sealing the fate of a 190 in one long burst. It could be strange to claim two types of aircraft in a single engagement, but the fact was that the Kiwis had engaged the new Ta152 which could be mistaken for a Bf109. The next day, only one patrol was flown but it would prove to be the most productive ever for 486. The squadron got airborne at 08.30 for an armed recce of the Müritzee Lake area. A formation of Fw190s was sighted a few miles south-east of Uelzen; when first seen, the Germans were to the right of 486 and flying a reciprocal course. Led by F/L Schrader, the Kiwis gave chase. At about 1000 yards, the Fw190s scattered and each member of the patrol selected a target. Schrader chose the aircraft on the extreme left of the formation and caught it during its turn. He fired from 300 yards and the Fw190 was immediately hit; having seen some pieces shedding from the aircraft, Schrader watched as it burst into flames, rolled on to its back and spiralled down in an almost vertical attitude. Joining the general melee, he soon sealed the fate of another Fw190. Schrader's wingman, W/O R.J. Atkinson got one more with a short burst that hit the cockpit. The Fw190 caught fire, then the nose dropped and the fighter was seen to plunge in flames into the middle of a forest. Flying Officer B.J. O'Connor claimed an Fw190 destroyed and one more damaged, while F/L A.I. Ross, F/O A.R. Evans, W/O G. Maddaford and F/Sgt R.A. Melles each claimed a Fw190 destroyed. It was an impressive score for the loss of just one Tempest; Evans was shot down but managed to bale out, rejoining the squadron later that day. The next day, the 16ᵗʰ, 486 continued to score, with an Fw190 destroyed near Neustadt in the morning, shared by Sheddan and Shaw, and, in the afternoon, Schrader and F/O J.W. Reid each claimed an Fw190 destroyed near Ludwigslust. Schrader was again in the headlines a few

Some of 486 Sqn in front of an Fw190 at Kastrup airfield near Copenhagen. The photograph was taken on 9 May 1945 by a photographer from the Danish daily paper Politiken.
Standing, left to right: F/L F.P. Kendall (British), F/Sgt J.W. Reid, W/O N.D. Howard, F/Sgt R.D. Roderick, W/O R.J. Atkinson, F/O C.J. MacDonald, P/O W.J. Shaw, W/O G. Maddaford, F/L B.S. Griffiths (British) and W/O R. Bird (British).
Squatting, left to right: F/Sgt R.A. Melles (†29.08.45 in a car accident), P/O H.T. Leach (British), F/O D.J. Thomson and F/L A.I. Ross. In the final weeks of the war, the lack of Kiwi pilots trained on Tempests obliged 2TAF to post in Australian and British pilots to replace losses and tour-expired departures.
(Melles family via P. Sortehaug)

days later when, on the 21st, he was promoted to squadron leader to take command of 486. His A Flight CO position was assumed by Sheddan. It was in this new position that Schrader made his next claim. Operating near the Parchim–Schwerin area, he and Evans caught two Bf109s preparing to land at Schwerin airfield. One of the Bf109s already had its wheels down and was flying slowly, making it easy prey. However, Schrader opened fire from half a mile to deter the pilot from landing. The German understood the message and pulled up into a tight climbing turn, attempting to escape his fate. Schrader had already closed in and fired from close range. The Bf109 continued to turn and, in a shallow dive, barely a mile to the south of the airfield, hit the ground, bounced back into the air and flipped over on its back before coming to rest. The aircraft had broken into several pieces but had not caught fire so Schrader and his No. 2 strafed it until it burned. Soon after, Evans spied a Fw190 heading towards Wismar airfield. He shot it down with a single burst from 300 yards. This impressive series of claims was cooled by the loss of F/Sgt W.W. May on the 24th when he was shot down by flak while attacking ground targets near Hamburg. Fortunately, although badly injured, he was captured. Four days later, F/O K.A. Smith distinguished himself by claiming an Me262 destroyed, the first jet claimed by the squadron since Stafford and Bremner's success the previous December. He got lucky when, during a patrol, he spotted two Me262s. He managed, with his wingman, to trail the two jets back to their airfield at Lübeck and caught one of them in the circuit. He was able to deliver two attacks and, when he left the scene, could see the jet had careered off the runway and that smoke and flames appeared to be coming from it. He didn't have time to celebrate much as, the following day, he was shot down by flak north of Uithiele while attacking METs. Damaged, he headed for home but was obliged to make a forced landing in a paddock near Hamburg. Smith was taken prisoner soon after and put in a prison cell in Hamburg itself. He was joined by Melles who was also shot down by flak in the area the next day. Their captivity was brief as they both escaped together and rejoined the squadron on 5 May. In the meantime, the unit had made another move and was now at B.150/Fassberg in Germany. On the 28th, late in the afternoon west of Plon, F/L J.W. Reid and F/O O.D. Eagleson claimed an aircraft they identified as a Ju352; the claim was confirmed but Intelligence altered the claim to a Ju52 after viewing the gun camera films. Both pilots remained convinced the aircraft they had attacked had been much larger than the ubiquitous Ju52. On the 29th, the Elbe, the last barrier facing the 21st Army Group before they met the Soviets, was crossed with relative ease at Lauenberg. Many patrols were flown to cover the bridgehead during the day. The Luftwaffe was at the rendezvous and many encounters occurred. Not much after midday, the first claim was made by the CO when he destroyed an Fw190. Ten minutes later, more hostile aircraft appeared, leading to a major dogfight which ended with two more Bf109s credited to Schrader (making three confirmed kills for him for the day), a third Bf109 shared with W/O N.D. Howard (who also claimed another as damaged), while Eagleson was good for one Fw190 destroyed and a second damaged, one Fw190 destroyed for F/O C.S. Kennedy and another probably destroyed by Evans. The squadron returned to the same area in the middle of the afternoon and another combat took place with the Luftwaffe; three more Fw190s were shot down, one each credited to Reid, F/O C.J. McDonald and W/O J.R. Duncan. That evening, during the last patrol of the day, Evans claimed a tenth victory for 486, his victim being a Bf109 which fell two miles south of Bergedorf. The month ended with another claim, a Bf109 claimed as damaged near Ludwigslust. Even with the war in Europe approaching its inevitable end, the rhythm of operations was maintained during the first days of May. More than 100 sorties were flown and activity remained intense. On 1 May, Schrader claimed a Bf109 shot down over Bad Segeberg, while, the next day, Eagleson, during the first armed recce of the day, saw an Fw44 flying on the deck seven miles south of Schwerin; he attacked and easily shot it down, the aircraft crashing in flames. The same pilot, during the next armed recce, saw an Fi156 on the ground and destroyed it as well. His luck eventually left him later in the evening when he was hit by flak while attacking a stationary train near Lübeck. Eagleson made an emergency landing in enemy territory but managed to escape capture and was back with the squadron two days later. He had made a good landing unscathed and was actually captured by German soldiers soon after. He escaped during a halt while retreating from British forces. In the meantime, during a previous armed recce, P/O W.J. Shaw and W/O N.D. Howard shared in the destruction of an Fi156 and a Fw190 south of Neumünster. The day was not over, however, as, very late in the evening, a final claim was made by Sheddan and F/O D.J. Thompson. Sheddan had just been promoted to lead 486 earlier in the day after Schrader was posted to command No. 616 Squadron, the first jet squadron in the RAF. Now Squadron Leader Sheddan was leading the formation for the last armed recce of the day in the Fulda area. Suddenly, he saw a German flying boat orbiting; he identified it as a multi-engine (possibly a Bv139) aircraft and attacked it from astern. He saw various strikes on the fuselage and the two right engines. Both engines streamed smoke and the flying boat lost height and landed on the water, swinging onto the beach. By this time, it had caught fire and was last seen with several explosions spreading debris across the beach. As Thompson had participated in the attack, the claim was shared. The last enemy aircraft to fall to 486's guns were two Ju88s shot down northwest of Jagel, the two victorious pilots being MacDonald and Duncan. May 3 was also a bad day for 486 as two Tempests were lost. The first was flown by P/O J.E. Wood; hit by flak, he had to put his Tempest down north-west of Neumünster. He was apprehended by a civilian who locked him up in a lavatory, but he managed to escape and rejoined the squadron ten days later. By that time, the war was over. In the late afternoon, it was the turn of F/O C.E. Blee to be shot down, being caught by flak over Hamburg while returning home. While he made a crash landing in a friendly sector, he suffered bad fractures in his back, skull and arm in the process. He would need a full year to recover before he was repatriated to New Zealand. These two pilots were not the squadron's last losses of the war. The next day, F/O T.M. Austin experienced engine trouble while attacking a Fi156 with several other pilots. While the Fi156 was finally destroyed on the ground, Austin was obliged to make a belly landing in an enemy-held sector and was immediately captured and taken to hospital with a broken wrist. He was eventually released on 10 May. The next day, the 5th, 486 carried out its last sorties of the war, an escort for Dakotas carrying Military Mission personnel to Copenhagen. Led by Sheddan, the escort took place between 17.15 and 19.45 and was completed without incident. Over the next few days, 486 made two moves: B.118/Celle in Germany on the 6th and B.160/Karup in Denmark two days later. Another move followed on 6 July, the squadron returning to Germany to be stationed at B.158/Lubeck until disbandment was announced on 7 September 1945. During this period of peace and rest, the squadron continued to fly many practice sorties. Some ended badly, like on 19 June when a wing panel flew off Eagleson's aircraft. He baled out into Copenhagen harbour and was rescued unscathed. Two months later, and two weeks before disbandment, P/O W.J. Shaw hit the sea while flying too low; while he managed to return to base, he crashed his Tempest and fractured his spine. His aircraft was not repaired and was struck off charge the following October.

Date	Pilot	SN	Origin	Type	Serial	Code	Nb	Cat.
				HURRICANE MK II				
23.07.42	F/L Harvey N. **SWEETMAN**	NZ40992	RNZAF	Do217	**Z3029**	SA-R	0.5	C
	Shared with a 409 Sqn crew							
				TYPHOON MK I				
17.10.42	P/O Gordon G. **THOMAS**	NZ403999	RNZAF	Fw190			0.5	C
	Sgt Arthur N. **SAMES**	NZ411453	RNZAF		**R8641**	SA-E	0.5	C
17.12.42	F/Sgt Francis **MURPHY**	NZ411928	RNZAF	Bf109	**R8744**	SA-M	0.5	C
	Sgt Keith G. **TAYLOR-CANNON**	NZ412284	RNZAF		**R8664**	SA-B	0.5	C
	F/Sgt Francis **MURPHY**	NZ411928	RNZAF	Bf109	**R8744**	SA-M	0.5	C
	Sgt Keith G. **TAYLOR-CANNON**	NZ412284	RNZAF		**R8664**	SA-B	0.5	C
18.12.42	P/O Gordon G. **THOMAS**	NZ403999	RNZAF	Do217	**R8681**	SA-E	0.5	C
	F/Sgt Russell W.S. **PENNY**	NZ404937	RNZAF		**R8800**	SA-L	0.5	C
19.12.42	Sgt Arthur N. **SAMES**	NZ411453	RNZAF	Fw190	**R8660**	SA-Y	1.0	C
22.12.42	F/O Arthur E. **UMBERS**	NZ404003	RNZAF	Do217	**R8697**	SA-Z	0.5	C
	F/Sgt Charles N. **GALL**	NZ411492	RNZAF		**R8800**	SA-L	0.5	C
24.12.42	F/O Gordon G. **THOMAS**	NZ403999	RNZAF	Bf109	**R8781**	SA-H	1.0	C
	F/Sgt Francis **MURPHY**	NZ411928	RNZAF	Bf109	**R8744**	SA-M	1.0	C
17.01.43	Sgt Keith G. **TAYLOR-CANNON**	NZ412284	RNZAF	Bf109	**R8781**	SA-H	0.5	C
16.02.43	F/Sgt Francis **MURPHY**	NZ411928	RNZAF	Ju88	**DN428**	SA-L	1.0	C
01.03.43	F/Sgt Wallis B. **TYERMAN**	NZ412008	RNZAF	Fw190	**DN303**	SA-P	1.0	C
14.03.43	F/Sgt Roderick H. **FITZGIBBON**	NZ411874	RNZAF	Fw190	**R8744**	SA-M	0.5	C
09.04.43	S/L Desmond J. **SCOTT**	NZ40779	RNZAF	Fw190	**EJ928**		0.25	P
	F/L Harvey N. **SWEETMAN**	NZ40992	RNZAF		**R8881**	SA-R	0.25	P
	F/L Arthur E. **UMBERS**	NZ404003	RNZAF		**EJ969**	SA-A	0.25	P
	F/O Ian D. **WADDY**	NZ402195	RNZAF		**R8684**	SA-B	0.25	P
14.04.43	S/L Desmond J. **SCOTT**	NZ40779	RNZAF	Bf109	**DN596**	SA-I	0.5	C
	F/Sgt Roderick H. **FITZGIBBON**	NZ411874	RNZAF		**R8781**	SA-H	0.5	C
16.04.43	*Squadron*	-	-	Bf109	**DN303**	SA-P	1.0	C
29.04.43	F/O Allan H. **SMITH**	NZ411947	RNZAF	Bf109	**DN428**	SA-L	1.0	C
	P/O Francis **MURPHY**	NZ411928	RNZAF	Bf109	**EJ969**	SA-A	1.0	C
25.05.43	S/L Desmond J. **SCOTT**	NZ40779	RNZAF	Bf109	**EJ928**		1.0	C
24.06.43	S/L Desmond J. **SCOTT**	NZ40779	RNZAF	Fw190	**EJ981**	SA-F	1.0	C
	F/L Arthur E. **UMBERS**	NZ404003	RNZAF	Fw190	**EK119**	SA-H	1.0	C
15.07.43	P/O Arthur N. **SAMES**	NZ411453	RNZAF	Fw190	**R8697**	SA-Z	1.0	C
	S/L Desmond J. **SCOTT**	NZ40779	RNZAF	Fw190	**EJ981**	SA-F	0.5	C
	F/Sgt Roderick H. **FITZGIBBON**	NZ411874	RNZAF		**DN332**	SA-D	0.5	C
	F/L Arthur E. **UMBERS**	NZ404003	RNZAF	Fw190	**EJ973**	SA-B	1.0	P
	P/O Francis **MURPHY**	NZ411928	RNZAF	Fw190	**DN369**	SA-C	1.0	P
				TEMPEST MK V				
16.06.44	F/Sgt Brian J. **O'CONNOR**	NZ402747	RNZAF	V-1	**JN809**	SA-M	1.0	C
	P/O Kevin **MCCARTHY**	NZ417075	RNZAF	V-1	**JN801**	SA-L	1.0	C
17.06.44	F/O Thomas M. **FENTON**	NZ422273	RNZAF	V-1	**JN808**	SA-N	1.0	C
	P/O Raymond J. **DANZEY**	NZ416464	RNZAF	V-1	**JN809**	SA-M	1.0	C

N.B: 150 Wing ORB gives 4 V-1s destroyed for 486 that day.

Claude Lyttleton Collingwood Roberts
RAF No. 37363

A pre-war RAF officer, Roberts joined the RAF in 1935. When war broke out, he was already a flight commander with No. 79 Squadron with which he participated in the Battle of France and covered the withdrawal from Dunkirk. Rested, he was sent to instruct, but was later posted sick; his subsequent medical category prohibited operational flying for 12 months. Therefore, he continued to instruct until his full medical status was restored at the beginning of 1942. In March, he was given command of the newly formed No. 486 (NZ) Squadron with the aim of bringing the unit up to operational standard. Roberts led the Kiwis until April 1943 when he left to command No. 257 (Burma) Squadron, also flying Typhoons, for the next two months. In May, he left 257 as a wing commander. No further operational positions were held before the end of the war.

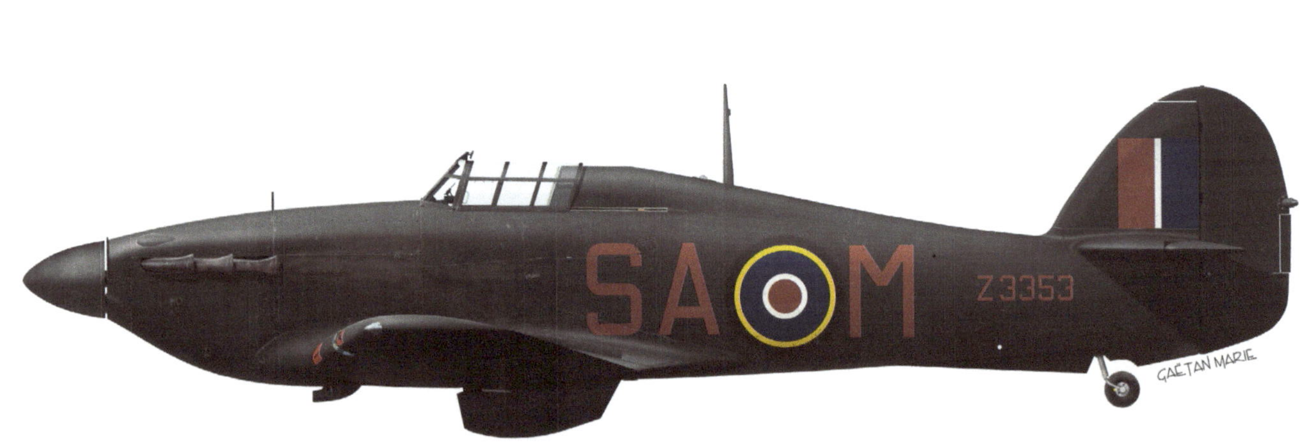

Hawker Hurricane Mk IIB Z3353
No. 486 (NZ) Squadron
Wittering (UK), spring 1942

Some 486 Squadron pilots who by the end of 1942 had scored over the German raiders, L-R, F/O G.G.Thomas (†09.04.43, CGS), F/Sgt F. Murphy, Sgt K.G. Taylor-Cannon (†13.04.5 as OC 486), Sgt A.N. Sames, F/O A.E. Umbers (†14.02.45 as OC 486), and F/Sgt C.N. Gall. Below, F/Sgt Murphy (left) with F/O A.H. Smith who put down two reconnaissance aircraft Bf109s on 29 April 1943. *(JH McCaw via P. Sortehaug - both)*

Francis MURPHY
NZ411928

'Spud' Murphy enlisted in the RNZAF in March 1941 and he undertook his initial training before being posted to the UK as an NCO. He attended 52 OTU and was then posted to 486 Squadron in March 1942. Flying initially Hawker Hurricanes, he switched to the Typhoon and claimed one of the first squadron's claims on the type on 17 December in claiming two Bf109 destroyed, he shared. He continued to score the following weeks and received his commission early in 1943. In May, he was awarded the DFC, the first awarded to the squadron. On 15 July 1943, he made his last claim, a Fw190 probably destroyed, sealing his tally to five confirmed victories, two being shared, and one probable. In September, he took a flight commander position, and he eventually completed his first tour in February 1944. He was posted to Hawkers as a production test pilot until the end of the war, and continued his career with Hawkers after the war.

Hawker Typhoon Mk IB R8697
No. 486 (NZ) Squadron
Wittering (UK), August 1942

Date								
18.06.44	F/O William A. **HART**	NZ424461	RNZAF	*V-1*	**JN797**	SA-K	1.0	C
	F/O Neville J. **POWELL**	NZ415013	RNZAF	*V-1*	**JN804**	SA-R	1.0	C
	F/Sgt Owen D. **EAGLESON**	NZ421689	RNZAF	*V-1*	**JN811**	SA-Z	1.0	C
	P/O Raymond J. **DANZEY**	NZ416464	RNZAF	*V-1*	**JN797**	SA-K	1.0	C
	F/O James G. **WILSON**	NZ403555	RNZAF	*V-1*	**JN809**	SA-M	1.0	C
	F/L Vaughan St.C. **COOKE**	NZ404898	RNZAF	*V-1*	**JN801**	SA-L	1.0	C
	F/Sgt Owen D. **EAGLESON**	NZ421689	RNZAF	*V-1*	**JN804**	SA-R	2.0	C
	F/Sgt Bevan M. **HALL**	NZ421705	RNZAF	*V-1*	**JN809**	SA-M	1.0	C
	F/Sgt Roland J. **WRIGHT**	NZ421131	RNZAF	*V-1*	**JN770**	SA-V	1.0	C
	F/O James R. **CULLEN**	NZ416462	RNZAF	*V-1*	**JN758**	SA-Y	1.0	C
	F/O Stamford S. **WILLIAMS**	NZ412297	RNZAF	*V-1*	**JN810**	SA-P	1.0	C
19.06.44	F/O William L. **MILLER**	NZ402208	RNZAF	*V-1*	**JN811**	SA-Z	1.0	C
	F/O Raymond J. **CAMMOCK**	NZ414723	RNZAF	*V-1*	**JN810**	SA-P	1.0	C
	F/Sgt John H. **STAFFORD**	NZ421783	RNZAF	*V-1*	**JN803**	SA-D	1.0	C
	F/L Harvey N. **SWEETMAN**	NZ40992	RNZAF	*V-1*	**JN754**	SA-A	1.0	C
	F/L James H. **McCAW**	NZ414311	RNZAF	*V-1*	**JN770**	SA-V	1.0	C
20.06.44	P/O Raymond J. **DANZEY**	NZ416464	RNZAF	*V-1*	**JN801**	SA-L	1.0	C
	F/Sgt John H. **STAFFORD**	NZ421783	RNZAF	*V-1*	**JN808**	SA-N	1.0	C
	F/L James H. **McCAW**	NZ414311	RNZAF	*V-1*	**JN758**	SA-Y	1.0	C
21.06.44	F/O Stamford S. **WILLIAMS***	NZ412297	RNZAF	*V-1*	**JN866**	SA-U	1.0	C
	N.B: 150 Wing ORB gives 3 V-1s destroyed for 486 that day.							
22.06.44	F/L James H. **McCAW**	NZ414311	RNZAF	*V-1*	**JN758**	SA-Y	1.0	C
				V-1	**JN808**	SA-N	1.0	C
	P/O Kevin **McCARTHY**	NZ417075	RNZAF	*V-1*	**JN801**	SA-L	2.0	C
	F/O William L. **MILLER**	NZ402208	RNZAF	*V-1*	**JN794**	SA-T	1.0	C
	W/O Garnet J. **HOOPER**	NZ431213	RNZAF	*V-1*	**JN809**	SA-M	0.33	C
	Shared with two Spitfires, possibly of 91 Sqn							
	F/L James H. **McCAW**	NZ414311	RNZAF	*V-1*	**JN821**	SA-H	1.0	C
	W/O Cornelius J. **SHEDDAN**	NZ412358	RNZAF	*V-1*	**JN809**	SA-M	1.0	C
	S/L James H. **IREMONGER**	RAF No. 33342	RAF	*V-1*	**JN808**	SA-N	1.0	C
	F/Sgt John H. **STAFFORD**	NZ421783	RNZAF	*V-1*	**JN803**	SA-D	1.0	C
23.06.44	P/O Raymond J. **DANZEY**	NZ416464	RNZAF	*V-1*	**JN797**	SA-K	1.50	C
	Second claim shared with a Tempest of 3 Sqn							
	P/O Frank B. **LAWLESS**	NZ411417	RNZAF	*V-1*	**JN859**	SA-S	1.0	C
	F/Sgt Bevan M. **HALL**	NZ421705	RNZAF	*V-1*	**JN809**	SA-M	1.0	C
	P/O Kevin **McCARTHY**	NZ417075	RNZAF	*V-1*	**JN754**	SA-A	2.0	C
	F/Sgt Owen D. **EAGLESON**	NZ421689	RNZAF	*V-1*	**JN794**	SA-T	1.0	C
	F/O William L. **MILLER**	NZ402208	RNZAF	*V-1*	**JN808**	SA-N	2.0	C
	F/O Raymond J. **CAMMOCK**	NZ414723	RNZAF	*V-1*	**JN810**	SA-P	0.5	C
	Shared with a Spitfire of 91 Sqn							
	W/O Cornelius J. **SHEDDAN**	NZ412358	RNZAF	*V-1*	**JN801**	SA-L	1.0	C
	F/Sgt Sydney J. **SHORT**	NZ42465	RNZAF	*V-1*	**JN810**	SA-P	1.0	C
	F/Sgt Owen D. **EAGLESON**	NZ421689	RNZAF	*V-1*	**JN794**	SA-T	0.5	C
	Shared with a Spitfire of 41 Sqn							
	F/O James R. **CULLEN**	NZ416462	RNZAF	*V-1*	**JN770**	SA-V	0.5	C
	Claim shared with a Tempest of 3 Sqn							
	W/O William A. **KALKA***	NZ415415	RNZAF	*V-1*	**JN801**	SA-L	1.0	C
	F/O Raymond J. **CAMMOCK**	NZ414723	RNZAF	*V-1*	**JN810**	SA-P	1.0	C
24.06.44	F/O Raymond J. **CAMMOCK**	NZ414723	RNZAF	*V-1*	**JN808**	SA-N	2.0	C
	P/O Kevin **McCARTHY**	NZ417075	RNZAF	*V-1*	**JN803**	SA-D	1.0	C
	N.B: 150 Wing ORB gives 5 V-1s destroyed for 486 that day.							
25.06.44	F/O Stamford S. **WILLIAMS**	NZ412297	RNZAF	*V-1*	**JN758**	SA-Y	1.0	C
	F/Sgt Sydney J. **SHORT**	NZ42465	RNZAF	*V-1*	**JN801**	SA-P	1.0	C
	F/O Raymond J. **CAMMOCK**	NZ414723	RNZAF	*V-1*	**JN804**	SA-R	1.0	C
	F/O James R. **CULLEN**	NZ416462	RNZAF	*V-1*	**JN770**	SA-V	2.0	C
	W/O Cornelius J. **SHEDDAN**	NZ412358	RNZAF	*V-1*	**JN854**	SA-G	1.0	C
	F/O Raymond J. **CAMMOCK**	NZ414723	RNZAF	*V-1*	**JN804**	SA-R	1.0	C
	F/O William A. **HART**	NZ424461	RNZAF	*V-1*	**JN809**	SA-M	1.0	C

Prior to joining the RNZAF in March 1940, Scott, nicknamed 'Scottie', had been a member of the Territorial Army. He undertook his pilot training in New Zealand before sailing, in October 1940, to the UK where he attended 56 OTU. During January 1941 he was posted to No. 3 Hurricane Squadron as an NCO. It wasn't until 7 August that he was able to open his score, claiming a Bf109 probable and another damaged. One of the squadron's flights was detached to Manston where it dabbled in night intruding over the Continent. In this role Scott became its prized pilot, being involved in the destruction of four enemy aircraft with others probably destroyed or damaged. For his success and leadership, he received a DFC in May 1942 followed by a Bar to this in September.

After a period of rest he was posted briefly to 198 Squadron, before being appointed OC No. 486 (NZ) Squadron at the beginning of April 1943. He had therefore risen from NCO to Squadron Leader in under nine months. Flying Typhoons he made additional claims, bringing his total to eight confirmed victories, three being shared, six probables, two being shared, and six aircraft damaged . The last of these was a Fw190 which he damaged on 24 September 1943. The very next day he left the squadron, with a DSO, to become Wing Co Flying of the Tangmere Wing. He led the wing until November when he was again taken off operations, taking charge of RAF Station Hawkinge.

During this rest period he was twice involved in pulling injured airmen from their crashed machines. In March 1944, as a Group Captain, he was given command of No. 123 Wing, equipped with Typhoons, and aged just 25, became the RNZAF's youngest Group Captain. His operational duties ceased in February 1945, when he relinquished command of the wing and he left the RNZAF in May 1947.

Hawker Typhoon Mk IB R8843
Tangmere Wing
Wing Commander DJ Scott
Tangmere (UK), autumn 1943

Hawker Typhoon Mk IB MN941
No. 123 Wing
Group Captain DJ Scott
B.53/Merville (France), September 1944

Two Typhoons used as personal mount by DJ Scott, above, R8843 as Wing Leader of the Tangmere Wing and below MN941 as OC No. 123 Wing one year later.
(CT Collection - both)

<u>Ian Dousland WADDY</u>
NZ402915

Enlisting in the RNZAF in August 1940, Waddy completed his initial training in New Zealand then sailed to Canada for advanced training, duly sailing to England at the end of the summer of 1941. He attended 61 OTU and was then posted to No. 603 (City of Edinburgh) Squadron at the end of the year. His stay was short, however, as he was posted as a founding member of No. 486 (NZ) Squadron in March 1942. His progression was slow and deliberate as he became a flight commander in July 1943. Previously, he had made his only claim of the war with a shared probable victory over an Fw190 on 9 April. Regarded as a good leader, he was promoted to command 486 in September but, shortly before the end of his tour, he relinquished his position in January for a rest. Soon after, in March, he was awarded the DFC.

Waddy returned to operations in the middle of August 1944 to command the Typhoon-equipped No. 164 (Argentine-British) Squadron equipped. However, his stay was short as he was shot down by flak north of Rouen less than two weeks later; captured, he spent the rest of the war as a prisoner.

Hawker Typhoon Mk IB JP532
No. 486 (NZ) Squadron
Tangemere (UK), summer 1943

Date	Pilot	Serial	Air Force	Type	Aircraft	Code	Score	C
26.06.44	F/L James H. **McCaw**	NZ414311	RNZAF	*V-1*	**JN758**	SA-Y	1.0	C
	N.B: 150 Wing ORB gives 4 V-1s destroyed for 486 that day.							
27.06.44	F/O Neville J. **Powell**	NZ415013	RNZAF	*V-1*	**JN866**	SA-U	1.0	C
	W/O John R. **Powell**	NZ413889	RNZAF	*V-1*	**JN866**	SA-U	1.0	C
	F/L Harvey N. **Sweetman**	NZ40992	RNZAF	*V-1*	**JN754**	SA-A	1.0	C
				V-1	**JN821**	SA-H	1.0	C
	W/O Garnet J. **Hooper**	NZ431213	RNZAF	*V-1*	**JN803**	SA-D	2.0	C
	F/O William L. **Miller**	NZ402208	RNZAF	*V-1*	**JN811**	SA-Z	1.0	C
	W/O Owen D. **Eagleson**	NZ421689	RNZAF	*V-1*	**JN794**	SA-T	0.5	C
	Shared with a Tempest of 3 Sqn							
	F/O William A. **Hart**	NZ424461	RNZAF	*V-1*	**JN803**	SA-D	1.0	C
	F/O Raymond J. **Cammock**	NZ414723	RNZAF	*V-1*	**JN794**	SA-T	1.0	C
28.06.44	F/O James G. **Wilson**	NZ403555	RNZAF	*V-1*	**JN866**	SA-U	1.0	C
	W/O Owen D. **Eagleson**	NZ421689	RNZAF	*V-1*	**JN859**	SA-S	1.0	C
				V-1	**JN854**	SA-G	1.0	C
	F/O Raymond J. **Cammock**	NZ414723	RNZAF	*V-1*	**JN810**	SA-P	1.0	C
	P/O Frank B. **Lawless***	NZ411417	RNZAF	*V-1*	**JN859**	SA-S	1.0	C
	F/Sgt Bevan M. **Hall***	NZ421705	RNZAF	*V-1*	**JN809**	SA-M	1.0	C
	F/Sgt Roland J. **Wright***	NZ421131	RNZAF	*V-1*	**JN804**	SA-R	1.0	C
	N.B: 150 Wing ORB gives 5 V-1s destroyed for 486 that day.							
29.06.44	P/O Raymond J. **Danzey**	NZ416464	RNZAF	*V-1*	**JN797**	SA-K	2.0	C
	P/O Robert D. **Bremmer**	NZ424417	RNZAF	*V-1*	**JN821**	SA-H	1.0	C
	F/L Harvey N. **Sweetman**	NZ40992	RNZAF	*V-1*	**JN821**	SA-H	1.0	C
	F/Sgt John **Steedman**	NZ422328	RNZAF	V-1	**JN821**	SA-H	1.0	C
	W/O Cornelius J. **Sheddan**	NZ412358	RNZAF	*V-1*	**JN809**	SA-M	1.0	C
	W/O Sydney J. **Short**	NZ42465	RNZAF	*V-1*	**EJ527**	SA-Q	2.0	C
	F/O James R. **Cullen**	NZ416462	RNZAF	*V-1*	**JN810**	SA-P	1.0	C
30.06.44	W/O Sydney J. **Short**	NZ42465	RNZAF	*V-1*	**JN810**	SA-P	1.0	C
	F/Sgt Bevan M. **Hall**	NZ421705	RNZAF	*V-1*	**JN821**	SA-H	1.0	C
	P/O Frank B. **Lawless**	NZ411417	RNZAF	*V-1*	**JN811**	SA-Z	1.0	C
	F/L Eric W. **Tanner**	NZ415037	RNZAF	*V-1*	**JN770**	SA-V	3.0	C
	W/O John H. **Stafford**	NZ421783	RNZAF	*V-1*	**JN801**	SA-L	1.0	C
	F/Sgt Bevan M. **Hall**	NZ421705	RNZAF	*V-1*	**JN854**	SA-G	1.0	C
	F/L Harvey N. **Sweetman***	NZ40992	RNZAF	*V-1*	**JN801**	SA-L	1.0	C
	N.B: 150 Wing ORB gives 10 V-1s destroyed for 486 that day.							
01.07.44	P/O Frank B. **Lawless**	NZ411417	RNZAF	*V-1*	**JN770**	SA-V	1.0	C
	F/O Raymond J. **Cammock**	NZ414723	RNZAF	*V-1*	**JN866**	SA-U	1.0	C
	W/O Cornelius J. **Sheddan**	NZ412358	RNZAF	*V-1*	**JN821**	SA-H	1.0	C
	F/L Lloyd J. **Appleton**	NZ415213	RNZAF	*V-1*	**JN873**	SA-W	1.0	C
03.07.44	P/O Robert D. **Bremmer**	NZ424417	RNZAF	*V-1*	**JN801**	SA-L	1.0	C
	F/O James R. **Cullen**	NZ416462	RNZAF	*V-1*	**JN863**	SA-R	1.0	C
	W/O Owen D. **Eagleson**	NZ421689	RNZAF	*V-1*	**JN873**	SA-W	1.0	C
	P/O Keith A. **Smith**	NZ403828	RNZAF	*V-1*	**JN801**	SA-L	2.0	C
	W/O Cornelius J. **Sheddan**	NZ412358	RNZAF	*V-1*	**JN805**	SA-E	1.0	C
04.07.44	F/O Henry M. **Mason**	NZ413104	RNZAF	*V-1*	**JN805**	SA-E	1.0	C
	F/O James R. **Cullen**	NZ416462	RNZAF	*V-1*	**JN770**	SA-V	1.0	C
	W/O Owen D. **Eagleson**	NZ421689	RNZAF	*V-1*	**EJ537**	SA-S	1.0	C
	W/O William A. **Kalka**	NZ415415	RNZAF	*V-1*	**JN809**	SA-M	2.0	C
	P/O Frank B. **Lawless**	NZ411417	RNZAF	*V-1*	**EJ537**	SA-S	1.0	C
	F/L Harvey N. **Sweetman**	NZ40992	RNZAF	*V-1*	**JN809**	SA-M	1.0	C
	P/O Robert D. **Bremmer**	NZ424417	RNZAF	*V-1*	**JN854**	SA-G	1.0	C
	F/O Neville J. **Powell**	NZ415013	RNZAF	*V-1*	**EJ527**	SA-Q	1.0	C
	W/O John H. **Stafford**	NZ421783	RNZAF	*V-1*	**JN854**	SA-G	2.0	C
	F/O Stamford S. **Williams***	NZ412297	RNZAF	*V-1*	**JN820**	SA-P	1.0	C
	F/O Henry M. **Mason**	NZ413104	RNZAF	*V-1*	**JN809**	SA-M	0.5	C
	Possibly shared with a Tempest of 56 Sqn							
	P/O Raymond J. **Danzey**	NZ416464	RNZAF	*V-1*	**JN805**	SA-E	1.0	C
05.07.44	W/O Cornelius J. **Sheddan**	NZ412358	RNZAF	*V-1*	**JN854**	SA-G	1.0	C

Some of the squadron's V-1 experts:
Above left, F/O R.J. Cammock. Before being posted to 486 Sqn in May 1944, he completed a tour with 485 and 253 Squadrons, initially in the UK and then in North Africa, returning to the UK in July 1943. He was killed in action on 6 October 1944. *(Cammock family via P. Sortehaug)*
Above right, F/O R.J. Danzey was posted to 486 as an NCO. He left in March 1945, tour-expired, and survived the war. *(R.J. Danzay via P. Sortheaug)*
Below, R.J. Cammock (right) chatting with W/O O.D. Eagleson. The latter arrived at 486 in November 1943 for flying duties and would remain with the squadron almost until the end of war. He was captured on 2 May 1945, evaded the next day, was recaptured later that day, and escaped again on the 4th!
(via P. Sortehaug)

Date	Name	No.	Force	Type	Serial	Code	Score	Cat
	W/C Roland P. **BEAMONT**	RAF No. 41819	RAF	*V-1*	**JN751**	R-P	1.0	C
	F/Sgt Brian J. **O'CONNOR**	NZ402747	RNZAF	*V-1*	**JN803**	SA-D	1.0	C
06.07.44	F/Sgt Brian J. **O'CONNOR**	NZ402747	RNZAF	*V-1*	**JN803**	SA-D	1.5	C
	Shared with a Tempest of 3 Sqn							
	W/O Owen D. **EAGLESON**	NZ421689	RNZAF	*V-1*	**JN873**	SA-W	1.0	C
	W/O Garnet J. **HOOPER**	NZ431213	RNZAF	*V-1*	**JN805**	SA-E	2.5	C
	Third claim shared with a Tempest of 3 Sqn							
07.07.44	F/L Harvey N. **SWEETMAN**	NZ40992	RNZAF	*V-1*	**JN801**	SA-L	0.5	C
	P/O Raymond J. **DANZEY**	NZ416464	RNZAF		**JN809**	SA-M	0.5	C
	F/L Harvey N. **SWEETMAN**	NZ40992	RNZAF	*V-1*	**JN803**	SA-D	1.0	C
	W/O Owen D. **EAGLESON**	NZ421689	RNZAF	*V-1*	**EJ527**	SA-Q	1.0	C
	F/O Raymond J. **CAMMOCK**	NZ414723	RNZAF	*V-1*	**JN873**	SA-W	1.0	C
	F/O James R. **CULLEN**	NZ416462	RNZAF	*V-1*	**EJ527**	SA-Q	1.0	C
	F/O Henry M. **MASON***	NZ413104	RNZAF	*V-1*	**JN732**	SA-I	1.0	C
	W/O Owen D. **EAGLESON**	NZ421689	RNZAF	*V-1*	**JN873**	SA-W	1.0	C
08.07.44	F/O James R. **CULLEN**	NZ416462	RNZAF	*V-1*	**JN770**	SA-V	1.0	C
	F/L James H. **McCAW**	NZ414311	RNZAF	*V-1*	**JN758**	SA-Y	4.0	C
	P/O Frank B. **LAWLESS**	NZ411417	RNZAF	*V-1*	**JN770**	SA-Y	2.0	C
09.07.44	F/O James R. **CULLEN**	NZ416462	RNZAF	*V-1*	**JN873**	SA-W	1.5	C
	Shared with a Tempest of 56 Sqn							
	W/O Garnet J. **HOOPER**	NZ431213	RNZAF	*V-1*	**JN821**	SA-H	2.0	C
11.07.44	*The claims made by 486 that day were not confirmed*							
12.07.44	W/O Owen D. **EAGLESON***	NZ421689	RNZAF	*V-1*	**EJ527**	SA-Q	1.0	C
	P/O Bevan M. **HALL**	NZ421705	RNZAF	*V-1*	**JN805**	SA-E	0.5	C
	Shared with a Tempest of 3 Sqn							
	F/L James H. **McCAW***	NZ414311	RNZAF	*V-1*	**JN770**	SA-V	1.0	C
	F/O Stamford S. **WILLIAMS**	NZ412297	RNZAF	*V-1*	**EN523**	SA-X	1.0	C
	P/O Bevan M. **HALL**	NZ421705	RNZAF	*V-1*	**JN821**	SA-H	1.0	C
	W/O William A. **KALKA**	NZ415415	RNZAF	*V-1*	**JN803**	SA-D	4.0	C
	F/Sgt James S. **FERGUSON**	RAF No. 1558633	RAF	*V-1*	**JN767**	SA-B	1.0	C
	F/L Lloyd J. **APPLETON***	NZ415213	RNZAF	*V-1*	**JN770**	SA-V	0.5	C
	shared with ???							
	F/L Eric W. **TANNER***	NZ415037	RNZAF	*V-1*	**EN528**	SA-P	0.5	C
	shared with ???							
13.07.44	F/O Henry M. **MASON**	NZ413104	RNZAF	*V-1*	**JN732**	SA-I	2.0	C
	P/O William A.L. **TROTT**	NZ417131	RNZAF	*V-1*	**JN866**	SA-U	1.0	C
	W/O Brian J. **O'CONNOR**	NZ402747	RNZAF	*V-1*	**JN866**	SA-U	1.0	C
14.07.44	F/L James H. **McCAW**	NZ414311	RNZAF	*V-1*	**JN758**	SA-Y	2.0	C
	W/O Owen D. **EAGLESON**	NZ421689	RNZAF	*V-1*	**EN523**	SA-X	1.0	C
	F/O Stamford S. **WILLIAMS**	NZ412297	RNZAF	*V-1*	**JN860**	SA-Z	1.0	C
	F/O Henry M. **MASON**	NZ413104	RNZAF	*V-1*	**JN732**	SA-I	0.5	C
	Shared with a Tempest of 56 Sqn							
	F/O James R. **CULLEN**	NZ416462	RNZAF	*V-1*	**JN770**	SA-V	1.0	C
15.07.44	F/L James H. **McCAW**	NZ414311	RNZAF	*V-1*	**JN860**	SA-Z	1.0	C
	W/O Garnet J. **HOOPER**	NZ431213	RNZAF	*V-1*	**JN803**	SA-D	1.0	C
16.07.44	P/O Bevan M. **HALL**	NZ421705	RNZAF	*V-1*	**JN821**	SA-H	0.5	C
	Shared with a Tempest of 3 Sqn							
	P/O Raymond J. **DANZEY**	NZ416464	RNZAF	*V-1*	**JN803**	SA-D	1.0	C
18.07.44	S/L James H. **IREMONGER**	RAF No. 33342	RAF	*V-1*	**JN763**	SA-F	0.5	C
	F/O James R. **CULLEN**	NZ416462	RNZAF	*V-1*	**JN770**	SA-V	0.5	C
	F/L Harvey N. **SWEETMAN**	NZ40992	RNZAF	*V-1*	**JN754**	SA-A	1.0	C
	F/O James R. **CULLEN**	NZ416462	RNZAF	*V-1*	**JN770**	SA-V	0.5	C
	Shared with a Tempest of 56 Sqn							
19.07.44	F/O Stamford S. **WILLIAMS**	NZ412297	RNZAF	*V-1*	**EJ523**	SA-X	1.0	C
20.07.44	P/O Robert D. **BREMMER**	NZ424417	RNZAF	*V-1*	**JN802**	SA-C	0.5	C
	W/O Garnet J. **HOOPER**	NZ431213	RNZAF	*V-1*	**JN797**	SA-K	0.5	C
21.07.44	F/L James H. **McCAW**	NZ414311	RNZAF	*V-1*	**JN758**	SA-Y	1.0	C

Some more of the squadron's pilots from the Tempest era:
Above left, F/L H.N. Sweetman completed a tour with 486 Sqn between March 1942 and July 1943, having previously served with 234 and 485 Squadrons from March 1941. He started a second tour with 486 in February 1944, leaving in September to command 3 Sqn (also flying Tempests). Above right, P/O B.M. Hall didn't get the chance to complete his first tour, begun in January 1944, as he was killed in action on 27.12.44.
Below left, F/L J.H. McCaw arrived at 486 in August during the early days of the Typhoon. He remained for the next two years and ended the war as a test pilot with D Napier & Sons, testing experimental engines. He survived the war. Below right, F/O B.J. O'Connor served with the squadron between December 1943 and May 1945.

Date	Name	No.			Aircraft	Code		
22.07.44	F/O Raymond J. **Cammock**	NZ414723	RNZAF	*V-1*	**JN863**	SA-R	1.0	C
	F/O James R. **Cullen**	NZ416462	RNZAF	*V-1*	**EJ537**	SA-S	1.0	C
	P/O Raymond J. **Danzey**	NZ416464	RNZAF	*V-1*	**JN801**	SA-L	1.0	C
	F/O James R. **Cullen**	NZ416462	RNZAF	*V-1*	**EJ523**	SA-X	1.0	C
23.07.44	P/O William A.L. **Trott**	NZ417131	RNZAF	*V-1*	**JN758**	SA-Y	2.0	C
24.07.44	F/L Lloyd J. **Appleton**	NZ415213	RNZAF	*V-1*	**JN863**	SA-R	1.0	C
	F/L Eric W. **Tanner**	NZ415037	RNZAF	*V-1*	**JN732**	SA-I	1.0	C
26.07.44	P/O Robert D. **Bremmer**	NZ424417	RNZAF	*V-1*	**JN803**	SA-D	1.0	C
	F/O William A. **Hart**	NZ424461	RNZAF	*V-1*	**JN732**	SA-I	1.0	C
	F/O Raymond J. **Cammock**	NZ414723	RNZAF	*V-1*	**EJ523**	SA-X	1.0	C
	F/L James H. **McCaw**	NZ414311	RNZAF	*V-1*	**JN770**	SA-V	1.0	C
	P/O Keith A. **Smith**	NZ403828	RNZAF	*V-1*	**JN803**	SA-D	1.0	C
	F/L Vaughan St.C. **Cooke**	NZ404898	RNZAF	*V-1*	**JN763**	SA-F	0.5	C
	Shared with a Tempest of 3 Sqn							
	F/O Raymond J. **Cammock**	NZ414723	RNZAF	*V-1*	**JN770**	SA-V	1.0	C
	F/O James R. **Cullen**	NZ416462	RNZAF	*V-1*	**JN770**	SA-V	1.0	C
	W/O John H. **Stafford**	NZ421783	RNZAF	*V-1*	**JN803**	SA-D	1.0	C
27.07.44	F/O William A. **Hart**	NZ424461	RNZAF	*V-1*	**JN754**	SA-A	0.5	C
	P/O Robert D. **Bremmer**	NZ424417	RNZAF		**JN803**	SA-D	0.5	C
	P/O William A.L. **Trott**	NZ417131	RNZAF	*V-1*	**JN763**	SA-F	1.0	C
	F/O Raymond J. **Cammock**	NZ414723	RNZAF	*V-1*	**EJ523**	SA-X	2.0	C
	F/L James H. **McCaw**	NZ414311	RNZAF	*V-1*	**JN770**	SA-V	1.0	C
	W/O Owen D. **Eagleson**	NZ421689	RNZAF	*V-1*	**EJ586**	SA-Z	1.0	C
	W/O Brian J. **O'Connor**	NZ402747	RNZAF	*V-1*	**JN801**	SA-L	1.0	C
	F/L James H. **McCaw**	NZ414311	RNZAF	*V-1*	**EJ523**	SA-X	1.0	C
28.07.44	P/O Frank B. **Lawless**	NZ411417	RNZAF	*V-1*	**JN770**	SA-V	2.0	C
30.07.44	F/L James H. **McCaw**	NZ414311	RNZAF	*V-1*	**EJ523**	SA-X	1.0	C
03.08.44	W/O Owen D. **Eagleson**	NZ421689	RNZAF	*V-1*	**JN808**	SA-N	2.0	C
	F/O Stamford S. **Williams**	NZ412297	RNZAF	*V-1*	**JN858**	SA-Y	2.0	C
	F/O William A. **Hart**	NZ424461	RNZAF	*V-1*	**JN732**	SA-I	1.0	C
	P/O Robert D. **Bremmer**	NZ424417	RNZAF	*V-1*	**JN767**	SA-B	1.0	C
	F/O Neville J. **Powell**	NZ415013	RNZAF	*V-1*	**JN808**	SA-N	1.0	C
04.08.44	W/O Owen D. **Eagleson**	NZ421689	RNZAF	*V-1*	**EJ528**	SA-P	1.0	C
	W/O Brian J. **O'Connor**	NZ402747	RNZAF	*V-1*	**JN801**	SA-L	1.0	C
	P/O Keith A. **Smith**	NZ403828	RNZAF	*V-1*	**JN821**	SA-H	3.0	C
05.08.44	F/O Henry M. **Mason**	NZ413104	RNZAF	*V-1*	**JN801**	SA-L	1.0	C
06.08.44	F/O James G. **Wilson**	NZ403555	RNZAF	*V-1*	**JN802**	SA-C	1.0	C
	W/O William A. **Kalka**	NZ415415	RNZAF	*V-1*	**EJ524**	SA-M	1.0	C
	P/O William A.L. **Trott**	NZ417131	RNZAF	*V-1*	**EJ528**	SA-P	1.0	C
	F/O Raymond J. **Danzey***	NZ416464	RNZAF	*V-1*	**JN803**	SA-D	0.5	C
	P/O Robert D. **Bremmer***	NZ424417	RNZAF	*V-1*	**EJ524**	SA-M	0.5	C
	F/O Raymond J. **Cammock**	NZ414723	RNZAF	*V-1*	**EJ523**	SA-Z	1.0	C
	N.B: 150 Wing ORB gives 6 V-1s destroyed for 486 that day.							
07.08.44	F/O Raymond J. **Cammock**	NZ414723	RNZAF	*V-1*	**JN863**	SA-R	1.0	C
09.08.44	F/L Harvey N. **Sweetman**	NZ40992	RNZAF	*V-1*	**EJ577**	SA-F	1.0	C
	F/L Lloyd J. **Appleton**	NZ415213	RNZAF	*V-1*	**JN808**	SA-N	1.0	C
15.08.44	W/O Owen D. **Eagleson**	NZ421689	RNZAF	*V-1*	**EJ635**	SA-T	0.5	C
	Shared with a Tempest of 3 Sqn							
	F/O Raymond J. **Cammock**	NZ414723	RNZAF	*V-1*	**EJ528**	SA-P	1.0	C
	F/L Keith G. **Taylor-Cannon**	NZ412284	RNZAF	*V-1*	**JN808**	SA-N	1.0	C
16.08.44	F/Sgt John **Steedman**	NZ422328	RNZAF	*V-1*	**EJ528**	SA-P	2.0	C
	F/L Harvey N. **Sweetman**	NZ40992	RNZAF	*V-1*	**JN732**	SA-I	1.0	C
	W/O Owen D. **Eagleson**	NZ421689	RNZAF	*V-1*	**EJ635**	SA-T	3.0	C
	P/O Keith A. **Smith**	NZ403828	RNZAF	*V-1*	**JN808**	SA-N	1.0	C
	F/O William L. **Miller**	NZ402208	RNZAF	*V-1*	**JN803**	SA-D	1.0	C
18.08.44	F/O Neville J. **Powell**	NZ415013	RNZAF	*V-1*	**EJ523**	SA-Z	1.0	C
19.08.44	F/Sgt William J. **Campbell**	NZ422366	RNZAF	*V-1*	**JN802**	SA-C	1.0	C
23.08.44	W/O Cornelius J. **Sheddan**	NZ412358	RNZAF	*V-1*	**EJ577**	SA-F	1.0	C

Date	Pilot	Serial	Air Force	E/A	Aircraft	Code	Score	
27.08.44	F/L James R. **Cullen**	NZ416462	RNZAF	*V-1*	**JN770**	SA-V	1.0	C
28.08.44	P/O William A.L. **Trott**	NZ417131	RNZAF	*V-1*	**JN863**	SA-R	1.0	C
29.08.44	W/O Brian J. **O'Connor**	NZ402747	RNZAF	*V-1*	**EJ577**	SA-F	1.0	C
	P/O Keith A. **Smith**	NZ403828	RNZAF	*V-1*	**JN770**	SA-V	1.0	C
	F/O Bevan M. **Hall**	NZ421705	RNZAF	*V-1*	**JN803**	SA-D	0.5	C
	Shared with a Tempest of 3 Sqn							
	F/O Raymond J. **Cammock**	NZ414723	RNZAF	*V-1*	**JN863**	SA-R	1.0	C
	P/O John H. **Stafford**	NZ421783	RNZAF	*V-1*	**JN803**	SA-D	1.0	C
31.08.44	W/O Brian J. **O'Connor**	NZ402747	RNZAF	*V-1*	**JN803**	SA-C	1.0	C
30.09.44	F/O Stamford S. **Williams**	NZ412297	RNZAF	Bf109	**EJ715**	SA-B	1.0	C
26.11.44	F/L Keith G. **Taylor-Cannon**	NZ412284	RNZAF	Ju188	**EJ606**	SA-U	0.5	C
	F/O Stamford S. **Williams**	NZ412297	RNZAF		**EJ577**	SA-F	0.5	C
	P/O John **Steedman**	NZ422328	RNZAF		**JN869**	SA-R	1.0	P
25.12.44	F/O John H. **Stafford**	NZ421783	RNZAF	Me262	**EJ787**	SA-J	0.5	C
	P/O Robert D. **Bremmer**	NZ424417	RNZAF		**EJ523**	SA-D	0.5	C
27.12.44	F/L Eric W. **Tanner**	NZ415037	RNZAF	Fw190	**EJ541**	SA-T	1.0	C
				Bf109			1.0	P
	F/L Keith G. **Taylor-Cannon**	NZ412284	RNZAF	Fw190	**EJ828**	SA-Z	1.0	C
	F/O Keith A. **Smith**	NZ403828	RNZAF	Fw190	**EJ711**	SA-Q	1.0	C
	P/O Sydney J. **Short**	NZ42465	RNZAF	Fw190	**JN808**	SA-N	1.0	C
01.01.45	S/L Arthur E. **Umbers**	NZ404003	RNZAF	Fw190	**EJ577**	SA-F	1.0	C
				Bf109			1.0	C
	F/O William A.L. **Trott**	NZ417131	RNZAF	Fw190	**EJ606**	SA-U	1.0	C
	P/O Garnet J. **Hooper**	NZ431213	RNZAF	Fw190	**EJ750**	SA-B	1.0	C
	P/O Cornelius J. **Sheddan**	NZ412358	RNZAF	Fw190	**EJ748**	SA-I	1.0	C
14.01.45	F/O Colin J. **McDonald**	NZ412706	RNZAF	Bf109	**EJ755**	SA-A	1.0	C
23.01.45	F/O Raymond J. **Danzey**	NZ416464	RNZAF	Fw190	**NV715**	SA-F	1.0	P
	S/L Arthur E. **Umbers**	NZ404003	RNZAF	Bf109	**NV715**	SA-F	1.0	C
	F/O John H. **Stafford**	NZ421783	RNZAF	Bf109	**EJ706**	SA-M	0.5	C
	W/O Anthony H. **Bailey**	NZ417146	RNZAF		**EJ750**	SA-B	0.5	C
02.02.45	F/O John H. **Stafford**	NZ421783	RNZAF	Do217	**EJ523**	SA-D	0.33	C
	F/O Robert D. **Bremmer**	NZ424417	RNZAF		**NV719**	SA-E	0.33	C
	P/O Cornelius J. **Sheddan**	NZ412358	RNZAF		**NV952**	SA-K	0.33	C
22.02.45	F/L John H. **Stafford**	NZ421783	RNZAF	Bf109	**NV971**	SA-L	1.0	C
	F/O Andrew R. **Evans**	NZ427480	RNZAF	Bf109	**EJ714**	SA-W	1.0	C
24.02.45	S/L Keith G. **Taylor-Cannon**	NZ412284	RNZAF	Bf109	**NV706**	SA-J	1.0	C
	F/L Neville J. **Powell**	NZ415013	RNZAF	Bf109	**NV763**	SA-N	1.0	C
06.04.45	F/O Cornelius J. **Sheddan**	NZ412358	RNZAF	Ju87	**EJ711**	SA-Q	2.0	C
10.04.45	F/L Warren E. **Schrader**	NZ411944	RNZAF	Fw190	**SN129**	SA-M	1.0	C
12.04.45	F/L John H. **Stafford**	NZ421783	RNZAF	Fw190	**SN129**	SA-M	1.0	C
14.04.45	F/O Cornelius J. **Sheddan**	NZ412358	RNZAF	Fw190	**SN129**	SA-M	1.0	C
	F/O Sydney J. **Short**	NZ42465	RNZAF	Fw190	**NV651**	SA-R	0.5	C
	W/O William J. **Shaw**	NZ424528	RNZAF		**NV753**	SA-J	0.5	C
15.04.45	F/L Warren E. **Schrader**	NZ411944	RNZAF	Fw190	**NV969**	SA-A	2.0	C
	F/L Arthur I. **Ross**	NZ424523	RNZAF	Fw190	**SN176**	SA-N	1.0	C
	F/O Brian J. **O'Connor**	NZ402747	RNZAF	Fw190	**SN129**	SA-M	1.0	C
	F/O Andrew R. **Evans**	NZ427480	RNZAF	Fw190	**NV988**	SA-Y	1.0	C
	W/O Reginald J. **Atkinson**	NZ428068	RNZAF	Fw190	**EJ739**	SA-W	1.0	C
	W/O Glen **Maddaford**	NZ4211710	RNZAF	Fw190	**EJ888**	SA-X	1.0	C
	F/Sgt Ross A. **Melles**	NZ422538	RNZAF	Fw190	**NV753**	SA-J	1.0	C
16.04.45	F/L Cornelius J. **Sheddan**	NZ412358	RNZAF	Fw190	**SN129**	SA-M	0.5	C
	P/O William J. **Shaw**	NZ424528	RNZAF		**NV753**	SA-J	0.5	C
	F/L Warren E. **Schrader**	NZ411944	RNZAF	Fw190	**NV969**	SA-A	1.0	C
	F/L John W. **Reid**	NZ2073	RNZAF	Fw190	**NV753**	SA-J	1.0	C
21.04.45	S/L Warren E. **Schrader**	NZ411944	RNZAF	Bf109	**NV969**	SA-A	1.0	C
	F/O Andrew R. **Evans**	NZ427480	RNZAF	Fw190	**SN136**	SA-V	1.0	C
25.04.45	F/O Keith A. **Smith**	NZ403828	RNZAF	Me262	**EJ711**	SA-Q	1.0	C
28.04.45	F/L John W. **Reid**	NZ2073	RNZAF	Ju52	**EJ697**	SA-H	0.5	C

Date	Name	Serial	Air Force	Type	Aircraft	Code	Score	Cat
	F/O Owen D. **Eagleson**	NZ421689	RNZAF		**SN136**	SA-V	0.5	C
29.04.45	S/L Warren E. **Schrader**	NZ411944	RNZAF	Fw190	**NV969**	SA-A	1.0	C
				Bf109	**NV969**	SA-A	2.5	C
	W/O Neil D. **Howard**	Aus. 409307	RAAF		**EJ659**	SA-I	0.5	C
	F/O Owen D. **Eagleson**	NZ421689	RNZAF	Fw190	**SN176**	SA-N	1.0	C
	F/O Colin S. **Kennedy**	Aus. 423245	RAAF	Fw190	**JN802**	SA-Y	1.0	C
	F/O Andrew R. **Evans**	NZ427480	RNZAF	Fw190	**SN136**	SA-V	1.0	P
	F/O Colin J. **McDonald**	NZ412706	RNZAF	Fw190	**SN176**	SA-N	1.0	C
	F/L John W. **Reid**	NZ2073	RNZAF	Fw190	**EJ659**	SA-J	1.0	C
	W/O James R. **Duncan**	NZ427022	RNZAF	Fw190	**JN802**	SA-Y	1.0	C
	F/O Andrew R. **Evans**	NZ427480	RNZAF	Bf109	**SN136**	SA-V	1.0	C
01.05.45	S/L Warren E. **Schrader**	NZ411944	RNZAF	Bf109	**SN136**	SA-V	1.0	C
02.05.45	F/O Owen D. **Eagleson**	NZ421689	RNZAF	Fw44	**SN176**	SA-N	1.0	C
	P/O William J. **Shaw**	NZ424528	RNZAF	Fi156	**NV753**	SA-J	0.5	C
	W/O Neil D. **Howard**	Aus. 409307	RAAF		**EJ739**	SA-W	0.5	C
	P/O William J. **Shaw**	NZ424528	RNZAF	Fw190	**NV753**	SA-J	0.5	C
	W/O Neil D. **Howard**	Aus. 409307	RAAF		**EJ739**	SA-W	0.5	C
	S/L Cornelius J. **Sheddan**	NZ412358	RNZAF	EA	**SN129**	SA-M	0.5	C
	F/O David J. **Thomson**	Aus. 436437	RAAF		**EJ659**	SA-J	0.5	C
03.05.45	F/L Colin J. **McDonald**	NZ412706	RNZAF	Ju88	**SN176**	SA-N	1.0	C
	W/O James R. **Duncan**	NZ427022	RNZAF	Ju88	**JN802**	SA-Y	1.0	C

Total: 85.5 + 242.33 V-1s

**Claim not mentioned in 486 ORB - possibly never confirmed.*

S/L C.J. Sheddan with his two flight commanders in May 1945. Left, F/L C.J. MacDonald and, right, F/L A.I. Ross.
(CT Collection)

James Henry IREMONGER
RAF No. 33342

Already serving with the RAF when war broke out, Johnny Iremonger had spent the early years of his career in the Far East, initially flying Hawker Audaxes as an army co-operation pilot with No 20 Squadron. With the outbreak of war with Japan, he switched to the fighter role and was posted, in January 1942, to No 5 Squadron, still flying Audaxes, as the unit was about to convert to the Curtiss Mohawk. A few weeks later, he was posted to command No 17 Squadron. He led 17 until December 1942 when he was posted to No 224 Group HQ as a wing commander. He returned to the UK in the summer of 1943 and started a new tour, reverting to squadron leader, initially posted as supernumerary to No 197 Squadron, a Typhoon unit, in October 1943 before joining No 486 (NZ) Squadron in January 1944 to supervise the unit's transition to the Tempest. He led the squadron during the V-1 campaign, claiming two destroyed (one shared) himself during the summer. Iremonger eventually left 486 in December 1944 for an HQ position and was awarded the DFC in January 1945. He remained in the RAF after the war.

Hawker Tempest Mk. V JN763
No. 486 (NZ) Squadron
Squadron Leader JH Iremonger
Newchurch (UK), June 1944

Arthur Ernest UMBERS
NZ404003

'Spike' Umbers joined the RNZAF in November 1940. Trained in Canada, he sailed for the UK during the summer of 1941 and completed his course at No 53 OTU. He was posted to No 74 (Trinidad) Squadron in April 1941. In March 1942, when the second RNZAF fighter unit in Britain, No 486 (NZ) Squadron, was formed, he was posted in. He did not open his score until December that year when he shared in a Do217 while flying a Typhoon. In September 1943, now a flight commander, he was sent for a rest, having completed his tour, and was awarded the DFC. He returned to operations in April 1944 as a flight commander, flying Tempests, with No 3 Squadron where he destroyed about nineteen V-1s (three of which were shared) and received a Bar to his DFC (in July). In December 1944, he was again posted to 486, but this time as OC. He claimed three confirmed victories in January 1945 alone to bring his total to five confirmed (one shared), two probables (one shared), three aircraft damaged (one shared) and about twenty V-1s destroyed. Sadly, on 14 February 1945, while conducting an armed reconnaissance over Germany, he was shot down by flak and killed.

Hawker Tempest Mk. V EJ627
No. 486 (NZ) Squadron
B.80/Volkel (Netherlands), December 1944

Date	Pilot	S/N	Origin	Serial	Code	Fate
Hurricane Mk II						
04.08.42	P/O Robert J. **Dall**	NZ41535	RNZAF	**BD728**	SA-X	-
Typhoon Mk I						
02.10.42	P/O Raymond I. **Philipps**	NZ402993	RNZAF	**R8663**	SA-N	†
16.10.42	Sgt David B. **Clark**	NZ412787	RNZAF	**R8698**	SA-O	-
25.10.42	F/Sgt Jesse **Pearse**	NZ40427	RNZAF	**R8814**		†
31.10.42	P/O Leslie V. **Weir**	NZ412294	RNZAF	**R8701**	SA-P	†
24.11.42	Sgt Leo **Walker**	NZ412290	RNZAF	**R7866**	SA-D	-
18.12.42	Sgt Russell W.S. **Penny**	NZ404937	RNZAF	**R8800**	SA-L	†
08.01.43	Sgt Peter C. **Fisher**	NZ413050	RNZAF	**R8941**	SA-X	**Inj.**
24.02.43	F/Sgt Roderick H. **Fitzgibbon**	NZ411874	RNZAF	**R8662**	SA-A	-
	F/Sgt Norman E. **Preston**	NZ41937	RNZAF	**R8616**	SA-J	-
01.03.43	F/Sgt Murray O. **Jorgensen**	NZ413086	RNZAF	**R8706**	SA-U	-
14.03.43	F/Sgt Roderick H. **Fitzgibbon**	NZ411874	RNZAF	**R8744**	SA-M	-
24.03.43	F/Sgt William K. **Mawson**	NZ411430	RNZAF	**EJ956**	SA-I	**PoW**
16.04.43	F/L Harvey N. **Sweetman**	NZ40992	RNZAF	**R8881**	SA-R	-
16.05.43	F/O Andrew A. **Brown**	NZ404886	RNZAF	**EJ969**	SA-A	†
29.05.43	F/Sgt David **Bennett**	NZ413531	RNZAF	**DN303**	SA-X	-
06.09.43	P/O Roderick H. **Fitzgibbon**	NZ411874	RNZAF	**EK119**	SA-H	†
16.09.43	F/Sgt David **Bennett**	NZ413531	RNZAF	**EJ976**	SA-V	†
	F/Sgt Murray O. **Jorgensen**	NZ413086	RNZAF	**EK225**	SA-N	†
	P/O Norman E. **Preston**	NZ41937	RNZAF	**JP485**	SA-M	†
24.09.43	F/Sgt Howard C. **Saward**	NZ411943	RNZAF	**EJ915**	SA-Y	**PoW**
03.10.43	F/Sgt Cornelius J. **Sheddan**	NZ412358	RNZAF	**JP676**	SA-J	-
10.11.43	P/O Wallis B. **Tyerman**	NZ412008	RNZAF	**JP914**	SA-J	†
21.12.43	F/Sgt Noel J.A. **Helean**	NZ414288	RNZAF	**JP845**	SA-H	†
31.12.43	F/O Raymond A. **Peters**	NZ404467	RNZAF	**JP532**	SA-T	†
14.01.44	F/O Gibson **Philp**	NZ412265	RNZAF	**JR329**	SA-R	†
10.02.44	F/Sgt William J. **Swinton**	NZ414698	RNZAF	**JP689**	SA-P	**PoW**
Tempest Mk V						
01.05.44	F/O James G. **Wilson**	NZ403555	RNZAF	**JN771**	SA-D	-
10.06.44	P/O Frank B. **Lawless**	NZ411417	RNZAF	**JN772**	SA-Q	-
22.06.44	F/O Thomas M. **Fenton**	NZ422273	RNZAF	**JN806**	SA-Q	-
28.06.44	P/O Frank B. **Lawless**	NZ411417	RNZAF	**JN859**	SA-S	-
	F/Sgt Roland J. **Wright**	NZ421131	RNZAF	**JN804**	SA-R	†
30.06.44	F/Sgt Sydney J. **Short**	NZ42465	RNZAF	**JN810**	SA-P	-
01.07.44	P/O Kevin **McCarthy**	NZ417075	RNZAF	**JN773**	SA-C	**Inj.**
03.07.44	F/O William L. **Miller**	NZ402208	RNZAF	**JN811**	SA-Z	-
04.07.44	F/O Stamford S. **Williams**	NZ412297	RNZAF	**JN820**	SA-P	-
05.07.44	W/O Cornelius J. **Sheddan**	NZ412358	RNZAF	**JN854**	SA-G	**Inj.**
20.07.44	F/Sgt Sydney J. **Short**	NZ42465	RNZAF	**EJ527**	SA-Q	-
23.07.44	P/O William A.L. **Trott**	NZ417131	RNZAF	**JN758**	SA-Y	-
24.07.44	W/O William A. **Kalka**	NZ415415	RNZAF	**JN809**	SA-M	-
	F/O Neville J. **Powell**	NZ415013	RNZAF	**JN860**	SA-J	-
31.07.44	P/O Alexander A. **Wilson**	NZ422336	RNZAF	**EJ586**	SA-Z	†

No. 486 Squadron pilots and personnel in front of and on the wings of a Typhoon. RAF Station Tangmere, July 1943.
On Propeller hub: F/O J.R. Cullen (PoW 04.05.45), P/O R.H. Fitzgibbon (†06.09.43), F/Sgt W.J. Swinton (PoW 10.02.44).
Standing on wing: Cpl N.S. Parkes (armourer), F/Sgt Rainbow (Fitter, UK), F/Sgt J.R. Powell (crouching, †08.10.44), F/O L.J. Appleton, P/O F. Murphy.
Sitting on wing: P/O A.N. Sames, F/Sgt M.O. Jorgensen (†16.09.43), P/O W.B. Tyerman (†10.11.43), F/O R.J. Dall (†04.07.45, 33 Sqn), F/O C.N. Gall, JA Froggatt,
F/Sgt B.C. Thompson, Sgt D.G. Fail, F/O N.W. Faircloth, P/O N.E. Preston (†16.06.43), P/O K. McCarthy, F/O R.J. Danzey.
Standing in front: W/O J.G. Wilson, S/L S.R Thomas (British, attached, PoW 05.09.43, 3 Sqn), F/L I.D. Waddy (PoW 25.08.44, 164 Sqn), S/L D.J. Scott (CO), F/O
A.H. Smith, F/L M. Lees (MO), F/Sgt H.C. Saward. *(via P. Sortehaug)*
Below, Typhoon era, L-R, F/Sgt Dave Bennett, one of the three casualties of 16 September 1943, F/Sgt Joe Helean killed on 21 December and W/O Keith Williams,
killed in a flying accident on 13 March 1944. *(via P; Sortehaug)*

Date	Pilot	Serial	Service	Aircraft	Code	Fate
10.08.44	F/O Raymond J. **CAMMOCK**	NZ414723	RNZAF	**JN866**	SA-U	-
17.08.44	F/Sgt James W. **WADDELL**	NZ422335	RNZAF	**JN805**	SA-E	†
25.08.44	F/L Eric W. **TANNER**	NZ415037	RNZAF	**EJ625**	SA-T	-
06.10.44	F/O Raymond J. **CAMMOCK**	NZ414723	RNZAF	**JN863**	SA-R	†
07.10.44	F/O William A. **HART**	NZ424461	RNZAF	**EJ535**	SA-E	**PoW**
	W/O Anthony H. **BAILEY**	NZ417146	RNZAF	**EJ704**	SA-M	-
22.12.44	F/L Stamford S. **WILLIAMS**	NZ412297	RNZAF	**EJ715**	SA-B	†
26.12.44	F/O Colin J. **McDONALD**	NZ412706	RNZAF	**EJ716**	SA-A	-
	P/O Brian J. **O'CONNOR**	NZ402747	RNZAF	**JN869**	SA-R	-
27.12.44	F/O Bevan M. **HALL**	NZ421705	RNZAF	**EJ627**	SA-E	†
13.01.45	S/L Arthur E. **UMBERS**	NZ404003	RNZAF	**EJ577**	SA-F	-
	P/O William A. **KALKA**	NZ415415	RNZAF	**EJ606**	SA-U	-
	F/L Lloyd J. **APPLETON**	NZ415213	RNZAF	**EJ752**	SA-H	**Inj.**
02.02.45	P/O Garnet J.M. **HOOPER**	NZ413231	RNZAF	**EJ787**	SA-L	**PoW**
08.02.45	F/L William L. **MILLER**	NZ402208	RNZAF	**EJ750**	SA-B	**PoW**
14.02.45	S/L Arthur E. **UMBERS**	NZ404003	RNZAF	**NV715**	SA-F	†
25.02.45	W/O Ronald C. **MacPHERSON**	NZ417222	RNZAF	**EJ523**	SA-D	**PoW**
25.03.45	F/O William A. **KALKA**	NZ415415	RNZAF	**NV981**	SA-A	†
26.03.45	P/O Anthony H. **BAILEY**	NZ417146	RNZAF	**NV932**	SA-U	†
13.04.45	S/L Keith G. **TAYLOR-CANNON**	NZ412284	RNZAF	**SN184**	SA-F	†
	F/Sgt Warren J.K. **HART**	NZ4211710	RNZAF	**EJ864**	SA-D	**Inj.**
14.04.45	W/O Owen J. **MITCHELL**	NZ424498	RNZAF	**SN141**	SA-U	†
15.04.45	F/O Andrew R. **EVANS**	NZ427480	RNZAF	**NV988**	SA-Y	-
24.04.45	F/Sgt Walter W. **MAY**	NZ44799	RNZAF	**NV651**	SA-R	**PoW**
26.04.45	F/O Keith A. **SMITH**	NZ403828	RNZAF	**NV967**	SA-Z	**PoW**
27.04.45	F/Sgt Ross A. **MELLES**	NZ422538	RNZAF	**EJ584**	SA-D	**PoW**
02.05.45	F/O Owen D. **EAGLESON**	NZ421689	RNZAF	**NV722**	SA-Q	**Eva.**
03.05.45	P/O John E. **WOOD**	NZ422339	RNZAF	**NV791**	SA-L	**PoW**
	P/O Charles E. **BLEE**	NZ438131	RNZAF	**EJ550**		**Inj.**
04.05.45	F/O Thomas McK. **AUSTIN**	NZ416896	RNZAF	**JN877**	SA-Y	**PoW**

Total: 72

Tempest EJ627/SA-E taking off during autumn 1944. This aircraft was shot down by Fw190s on 27 December 1944. Flying Officer B.M. Hall was killed.
A fitter working on EJ752/SA-H paused to warm his hands over a brazier at B.80/Volkel. Conditions for groundcrew were harsh during the winter of 1944/45 when most maintenance had to be carried out in the open. *(CT Collection)*

Keith Granville TAYLOR-CANNON
NZ412284

'Hyphen' spent his wartime career with No 486 (NZ) Squadron. He enlisted in the RNZAF in April 1941 and, on completion of training in March 1942, was posted to 486 as an NCO. He made his first claim on 17 December when he destroyed two Bf109s he shared. Commissioned, he was awarded a DFC in March 1944 at the end of his first tour. He returned to 486 in August to command B Flight, eventually being promoted to command in February 1945. Soon after, on the 24th, he made his final claim with a Bf109 destroyed over Germany. His tally by then consisted of five confirmed victories (one shared), one shared probable and one V-1. Taylor-Cannon commanded 486 for two months until he was shot down and posted missing on 13 April. He had been awarded a Bar to his DFC the previous month.

Hawker Tempest Mk. V NV986
No. 486 (NZ) Squadron
Squadron Leader KG Taylor-Cannon
B.80/Volkel (Netherlands), March 1945

Left, EJ712/SA-T photographed at Volkel in early October 1944. The D-Day stripes were at the time applied under the fuselage only. *(CT Collection)*

Middle left, The opposite side of NV753/SA-J, see p15. *(CT Collection)*

Below, photo taken from F/l J.W. Reid's cockpit of a section about to scramble at Kastrup. In the nearest Tempest JN807/SA-U with F/L F.P. Kendall on board (British) and behind EJ888/SA-X with P/O J.R. Duncan. *(JR Reid via P. Sortehaug)*

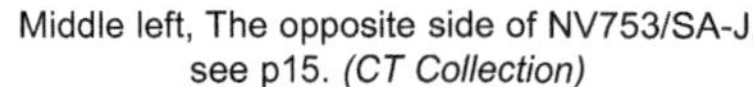

Some Tempests that participated to the V-1 campaign. Above EJ560/SA-M and, below, JN802/SA-Y. At the time, JN804 was coded 'SA-C'. JN802 left 486 Sqn in November 1944 and returned at the end of April 1945 to be coded 'SA-Y'. *(P. Sortehaug)*

Warren Edward Schrader
NZ411944

'Smoky' Schrader joined the RNZAF in March 1941. Following training in New Zealand, Canada and the UK, he was posted as an NCO to 165 Squadron in April 1942. He was commissioned and remained with the squadron until the end of the year. During February 1943, he left for an overseas posting and, by March, was serving with 1435 Squadron, operating Spitfires, on Malta, later moving with the unit to Italy. He had been appointed a flight commander, during July while on Malta, but it wasn't until being based in Italy that he made his first claims. In November, he destroyed an Italian bomber on the ground and, on 17 December, scored a double kill by shooting down two Bf109s. He shared in shooting down another fighter on 3 January 1944 and was awarded the DFC in April, his tour ending the following month. He was rested and served as a flying instructor until returning to the UK at the beginning of 1945. He transitioned to the Hawker Typhoon and Tempest and joined 486 in March, taking over the squadron in April, succeeding S/L Taylor-Cannon. That month was to be a very successful one with Schrader making nine claims in three weeks. On 1 May, he scored his last aerial victory, a Bf109, to bring his total to thirteen confirmed victories (two shared). The next day, he was promoted to wing commander and given command of 616 (South Yorkshire) Squadron to fly Gloster Meteor jets. In the week preceding VE-Day, he managed to destroy three German aircraft on the ground. He was awarded a Bar to his DFC, left 616 n August, and the RNZAF in December 1946.

Hawker Tempest Mk. V NV969
No. 486 (NZ) Squadron
Squadron Leader WE Schrader
B.80/Volkel (Netherlands), April 1945

Date	Pilot	S/N	Origin	Serial	Code	Fate
	HURRICANE MK II					
02.05.42	F/Sgt Gerald E. **RAWSON**	NZ404943	RNZAF	**Z3646**	SA-V	-
15.07.42	P/O Ian Hamilton **IRVINE**	NZ402191	RNZAF	**BD725**	SA-J	†
	TYPHOON MK I					
31.10.42	P/O Robert J. **DALL**	NZ41535	RNZAF	**R8801**	SA-X	-
03.08.43	F/O Charles N. **GALL**	NZ411492	RNZAF	**R8697**	SA-Z	-
	Sgt John R. **POWELL**	NZ413889	RNZAF	**DN611**	SA-V	-
20.11.43	*Destroyed by fire while in an hanger*	-	-	**JR501**	SA-R	-
	Destroyed by fire while in an hanger	-	-	**JP853**	SA-K	-
	F/Sgt Noel J.A. **HELEAN**	NZ414288	RNZAF	**EJ981**	SA-E	-
13.03.44	W/O Harry K. **WILLIAMS**	NZ414721	RNZAF	**JR146**	SA-M	†
05.04.44	F/Sgt Alfred G. **TURNER**	NZ412288	RNZAF	**JP839**	SA-V	†
	TEMPEST MK V					
27.04.44	F/O Henry M. **MASON**	NZ413104	RNZAF	**JN792**		-
19.06.45	F/O Owen D. **EAGLESON**	NZ421689	RNZAF	**NV969**	SA-A	-
27.08.45	P/O William J. **SHAW**	NZ424528	RNZAF	**EJ659**	SA-I	**Inj.**

Total: 13

Typhoon EJ948/SA-Z seen at its dispersal. Its undersurfaces are painted with the identification markings chosen for the Typhoon to avoid to be taken for a Fw190 by the British Army AA gunners. (*via P. Sortehaug*)

Cornelius James Sheddan
NZ412358

'Jimmy' Sheddan joined the RNZAF in April 1941. He was trained in New Zealand and sailed to the UK in January 1942. He was initially at Hullavington, before completing his training at 57 OTU, and at the end of September joined.485 (NZ) Squadron as an NCO. However his stay was short for in January 1943 he was transferred to No.1 Delivery Flight. In May he returned to operations being posted to No. 486 (NZ) Squadron, equipped with Typhoons. He was shot down by flak once on 3 October but was picked up after spending 19 hours in the Channel. In spring, 1944, 486 Squadron converted to Tempests and was soon employed in the V-1 hunt. In one fortnight, during June and July, he would claim 7 destroyed, one being shared, but had to crash-land. He was hospitalised for a month returning to the unit in time to claim another V-1. He was held back through illness when the squadron moved to the Continent, but did join them later in November. He opened his score on 1 January 1945 shooting down a Fw190, followed by more successes in February and April. He was promoted a flight commander, and awarded a DFC during May. On 2 May he was given command of the squadron, the same day that he made his last claim, a four-engine flying boat, which was shared. His score of seven confirmed victories included three which were shared, in addition to his eight V-1s (one shared), He continued command of the squadron until it was disbanded in September 1945, and left the RNZAF in April 1946.

Hawker Tempest Mk. V SN129
No. 486 (NZ) Squadron
Squadron Leader CJ Sheddan
B.158/Lübeck (Germany), summer 1945

'Jimmy' Sheddan in his last mount, SN129/SA-M.

SQUADRONS! - The series

Donald James Matthew BLAKESLEE DFC

Supermarine Spitfire Mk.VB EN951
No. 133 (Eagle) Squadron
Flight Lieutenant D. J. M. Blakeslee
USN, J-4351
Gravesend (U.K), August 1942

Charles Cuthbertson LEARMONTH DFC*

Douglas Boston Mk. III A28-9 (ex A1.891)
No. 22 Squadron RAAF
Squadron Leader C. C. Learmonth
(7439)
Port Moresby (New Guinea), spring 1943

Hans Anton MAURENBRECHER

Curtiss P-40N-35-CU Cp 560
No. 120 (NEI) Squadron
Major H. Maurenbrecher
Biak (New Guinea), 1945-1946

Roland Prosper BEAUMONT DSO* DFC*

Hawker Tempest Mk.V JN751
No. 150 Wing
Wing Commander R. P. Beaumont
RAF No. 40800
Bradwell Bay (U.K), April 1944

Ronald Thomas SUSANS DSO DFC

North American P-51D-25-NT A68-724
No. 77 squadron, RAAF
Squadron Leader R. T. Susans
(74301)
Iwakuni (Japan), 1947

James Henry LACEY DFM*

Supermarine Spitfire Mk.XIV RN135
No. 17 Squadron
Squadron Leader J. H. Lacey
RAF No. 117798
Seletar (Singapore), autumn 1945

Introducing's RAF In Combat and Bravo Bravo Aviation's collection of highly-detailed and historically accurate, high-quality aviation prints. For more information on available prints, please visit :

www.RAF-IN-COMBAT.com

or

Prints available for this book: